D1423327

WEST COUNTRY HISTORIC HOUSES
AND THEIR FAMILIES

Compton Wynyates

WEST COUNTRY HISTORIC HOUSES AND THEIR FAMILIES

Volume Three
The Cotswold Area

ERIC R. DELDERFIELD

Illustrated with photographs taken by the author

DAVID & CHARLES : NEWTON ABBOT

0 7153 6089 2

Set in 10 on 11pt Plantin
and printed in Great Britain
by W J Holman Limited Dawlish
for David & Charles (Holdings) Limited
South Devon House Newton Abbot Devon

CONTENTS

INTRODUCTION

The Cotswolds are an area of great beauty, characterised by honey-coloured stone, great churches, tidy villages and prosperous towns, and over the centuries these lovely hills and valleys have been witness to a great cavalcade of history.

In the Cotswolds, the Romans built their great Fosse Way and for four hundred years it echoed to the marching feet of their legions. Centuries later the wide uplands became great sheep walks and the wool they produced provided a high proportion of the national income. The final battle of the bitter, seemingly endless Wars of the Roses was fought on the bloody meadow by Tewkesbury.

The Civil War of the seventeenth century was perhaps more devastating to the Cotswolds than anything that had gone before. Many skirmishes and battles took place there and castles, including Berkeley, Broughton and Sudeley, were beseiged and captured. Prisoners were incarcerated in some of the churches, great houses were pillaged and some were utterly destroyed.

Kings and queens, princes and abbots, statesmen and politicians, good, bad and indifferent, have formed part of the Cotswold scene for centuries, and there is still much to remind us of them and of the events in which so many played a major role. Who can visit Sudeley Castle and fail to be moved by the remains of the great fifteenth-century banqueting hall, or the corridors and rooms in the castle which Katherine, the surviving queen of Henry VIII, knew so well and where the final act of her unfortunate story was played out?

At Broughton Castle the plot took shape which ended in the confrontation with Charles I, and led eventually to his death on the scaffold.

The great pile of Berkeley Castle casts the memory even farther back and one is irresistibly drawn to the tragic scene of the murder of Edward II, which took place seven hundred years ago.

The human drama of the Civil War comes to mind again at Compton Wynyates, where lived the second Earl who, together with his six sons, took part in the battles of the time, including that of Edgehill, just six miles from their home.

At Dodington, there is a vivid reminder of the slave trade, a record as well set out and documented as anywhere in the kingdom.

And what men they who occupied these houses. Thomas Berkeley fought at Bannockburn when seventy years of age; John Fortescue, one of England's greatest chancellors, was also seventy when he followed his king on to the field at Towton and ten years later was present at the battle of Tewkesbury. Only when all the fighting was done did he retire to his home at Ebrington.

These people, and many more, are identified with the houses visited in these pages and it is no less interesting to follow the fortunes of the buildings themselves. Some at one time or another were neglected and fell into ruin or decay, but happily were rescued and rehabilitated before it was too late. The majority of those described in this book have been lived in continuously for centuries and most of them are family homes still. Those that are open to the public receive thousands of visitors each year, enabling them to marvel at the galaxy of talent which combined to design, build, decorate and furnish them. There is a gargantuan shovel-board at Stanway cut from an oak tree grown on the estate. Huge as it is, not a single join mars the surface. The superb interior decoration at Barnsley Park, the great double staircase at Dodington, Chastleton's covered plasterwork ceiling, and the amazing wall coverings at Owlpen are but some of these masterpieces.

The contribution these houses have made to Britain's culture is immeasurable and while their various owners may have differed in every other respect, they had in common a deep affection for the house in which they lived and successors who accepted their heritage and improved it for later generations—and, incidentally, for all of us who care to visit them.

The great architectural conceptions, the beauty wrought in timber, plaster and stone, the glorious pictures, works of art and exquisitely designed furniture, often handed down from generation to generation, are further enhanced by the fascinating stories attached to them, and the insight they afford into not only how their owners lived, but often what they thought.

Then, too, there are the grounds and gardens: the avenues at Blenheim, the clipped yews of Compton Wynyates and Sudeley, and the delightful parklands of Barnsley and Williamstrip. All reminders of a gracious way of life that is fast receding and all well worth a visit in their own right.

This is the third volume of *West Country Historic Houses and their Families*. The first embraced a selection from Devon, Cornwall and Somerset, the second was concerned with North Somerset, Wiltshire and Dorset. The present volume explores the Cotswolds area, and though the boundaries of the true Cotswolds are usually accepted as being from Meon Hill above Chipping Campden in the north, Tetbury in the south, Burford in the east and Wootton-under-Edge to the west, the limits have here been extended slightly to include places just beyond.

The wealth of lovely houses in this area has not made selection easy, but from Owlpen, tiny and compact, to great and sombre Berkeley, each has its own fascinating story. And in an endeavour to meet some kindly criticism of the two previous volumes, this time more has been written about each house, though there are fewer of them.

Many of the houses have their own private chapel but usually there is a village church standing close by and sometimes, as at Compton Wynyates, the history of the family is indivisible from the church. Here the battle honours of early wars rest above the sword owned by a man who fell in the first world war. At Stowell there are wall paintings in the church which leave us in no doubt as to the conception of hell in the minds of those artists of over eight hundred years ago. These family churches are not comparable with the great wool churches which are justly famous in their own right, but they nonetheless exemplify the faith and piety of past generations who lived perhaps even closer to death than we in the twentieth century.

Of the fifteen houses featured in the following pages, thirteen are still privately-owned and one is in the hands of the National Trust. Another is owned by the Ditchley Foundation. Eight of the houses, or their gardens, are open to the public at certain periods of the year.

I have had the privilege of visiting and photographing every one of the houses described and would like to take this opportunity of recording my sincere thanks for the assistance and unfailing courtesy I received. Sadly, since these accounts were written, two most charming owners have died: Lady Violet Benson of Stanway House and Mr Mark Dent-Brocklehurst of Sudeley Castle.

I would be churlish if I did not also express my gratitude to members of the library service in many parts of the country for their help in tracing elusive information and establishing various facts.

Penshurst
EXMOUTH   E. R. DELDERFIELD

BARNSLEY PARK

GLOUCESTERSHIRE

A superb Georgian baroque mansion

The village of Barnsley lies three miles from Cirencester and there still stands the lovely Barnsley House, built in 1697 and for several generations the home of the Bouchier family.

It was an heiress of that family who, in 1719, married Henry Perrot. Through her mother she was a niece of the first Duke of Chandos. A year later Henry Perrot started to build the mansion which stands in and takes its name from Barnsley

Park. Little is known as to the identity of the architect or decorators, though John Price is generally thought to have been the designer. The Perrots lived in the house until his death in 1740, by which time he had become Member of Parliament for North Oxfordshire.

Set in four hundred acres of fine parkland, this superb Georgian baroque mansion comprises two storeys and an attic storey, and gives the impres-

The imposing and beautifully proportioned south front

Two tiers of arches form an inner hall of equal height

sion of being much larger than it actually is. The west (entrance) front has nine bays, the three in the centre projecting, and four great Corinthian pilasters support a cornice. The beautiful golden Cotswold stone which was used for the building came from the local Barnsley quarry, Quarry Hill, which ceased working many years ago.

On entering the house, it is surprising to find that the hall entirely fills the centre of the two-storey front. The depth, however, is reduced by two tiers of arches forming an inner hall of equal height, bridged by a gallery with wrought-iron balustrades. The design here generally follows the exterior in the use of arches and a Corinthian order but on a smaller scale and surmounted by similar attic pilasters.

The ceiling of the hall has a plaster relief of Diana and Cupid encompassed by classical reliefs. A magnificent chimneypiece is believed to have been the work of Charles Stanley, who was a pupil of Peter Scheemakers.

Alcove niches in the lower part of the inner hall contain busts, one of which is believed to be a likeness of Andrea Palladio, the Italian architect. The other is thought to portray the eighteenth-century artist, Sir James Thornhill. Here, too, is a fine ceiling with the central figure of a cloud-borne goddess. Classical reliefs feature the gods, Plenty

Ceiling centrepiece of the inner hall

Diana and Cupid is the motif of the outer hall ceiling

and Wisdom, between seasons represented by children, and the busts of two philosophers stand on pedestals. The staircase, which gives on to an unusual half-landing, is stuccoed with medallions of the Virtues and other ornamentation.

A feature of the dining-room is a fireplace of the purest Adam style, with a central bas-relief depicting a classical sacrifice, and the drawing-room contains a fine collection of water colours by Peter de Wint. The present owner's aunt was his pupil, which is how the pictures came to Barnsley Park.

In 1807, John Nash extended the east front of the house and inserted a large central bay. The library was remodelled to contain it, making a large and attractive room. It was redecorated at the same time and is a fine example of the Etruscan style of interior decoration, invented and introduced by Robert Adam. The motifs were derived from copies of the Etruscan vases and urns made popular at the time by Josiah Wedgwood. The fireplaces are a feature of most of the rooms, the one in the library being a particularly fine specimen.

The wallpaper of the music-room has a base design of trees, and on to this Le Roy Hobden painted, in oils, birds in their natural colours and in a variety of lifelike poses. Beautiful in design, it is also unique in effect.

When the extensions were made to the house in 1807 the rooms on the first floor above the library had to conform to the new shape. As a result, they are of unusual proportions, but nonetheless attractive, and one of the dining-rooms on this floor has a fine chimneypiece dated about 1730. As part of the alterations at this time, Nash also designed the orangery close to the east front which produces a prolific crop of oranges all the year round.

One of the treasures of the house is a needle-

14

work miniature of Charles I, said to have been worked from the king's own hair. The memento has been handed down and carries the inscription:

Worked by ladies of the Carnwath family after the execution 1649.
Let this trifling memento of those troublous times be kept by the eldest member of the family, the Earl of Carnwath or my eldest son.

The Carnwath family died out some ten years ago, and the miniature will now remain at Barnsley Park.

The house is exposed on three sides and in the Victorian period every effort was made to obtain complete seclusion from the staff and offices. A wall was built at right angles to the house at the exposed (north) end, thus completely screening the house. By this wall are a number of stone memorials to household pets of various owners over the years.

Rare now, but quite usual in those days, is the washing green behind the wall, a spacious lawn surrounded by buildings. The laundry itself, complete with a row of deep sinks and capacious chimneys over the coppers, is quite a large building and must have been a most efficient unit. Close by was an ironing-room and a number of other smaller buildings for ancillary purposes. Large staffs were needed to run such establishments and indeed, up until 1957, fourteen people worked in the house, including a house carpenter and also a mason. The capacious Cotswold-tiled barn bears the date 1795, and nearby there is a walled kitchen-garden some two-and-a-half acres in extent. When work was being carried out there recently a large drain discovered in the centre of the garden was traced back to the cowsheds, an early and practical

A corner of the library showing the Etruscan decoration

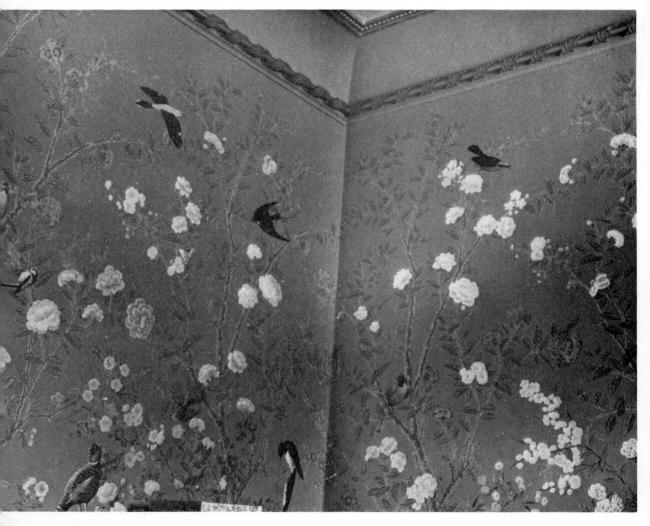

The unique and beautifully-patterned wallpaper in the music room

method of putting the manure to use in the right place.

During the second world war part of the Park was taken over by the Royal Air Force and it says something for the quality of their building that the stables lent themselves admirably to conversion into a very satisfactory officers' mess.

When Henry Perrot died in 1740, he left one daughter, Cassandra, and when she died, un-married, in 1778, Barnsley was bequeathed to a distant cousin, James Musgrave, who was then twenty-seven years of age and later succeeded to the family baronetcy. He died in 1814, and when the line ended with the death of the tenth baronet, Mr W. H. Wykeham-Musgrave inherited the property.

When Barnsley Park was sold to Lady Violet Henderson, grandmother of the present owner, most of the original furnishings were dispersed. Lady Henderson lived there until her death in 1957, and Lord Faringdon occupied the house until 1961, when it was purchased by his nephew, Mr C. M. Henderson, the present owner.

The estate, which is a farm of permanent grass, comprises 410 acres, including the great park with its fine vistas and avenues of majestic trees. For the past few years, Dr Graham Webster and his assistants from Birmingham and Bristol universities have been excavating on this land which has not been ploughed since Roman times and the discoveries they have made about the early field systems and about farm and domestic development over the ages have filled many gaps in our knowledge.

Mr and Mrs C. M. Henderson have three sons and one daughter.

A view of the outer hall

The overmantel in the hall

BERKELEY CASTLE

GLOUCESTERSHIRE

A medieval stronghold perfectly preserved

For more than eight hundred years Berkeley Castle has been in the same family and in those eight centuries it has been associated with almost every important phase of English history. The deeds, good and bad, which have been perpetrated within its sturdy walls are numberless. Here, one of the foulest of all murders took place, but here, too, great men were given encouragement and useful patronage in their studies, the results of which have benefited all mankind. William Harvey, pioneer in the study of the circulation of the blood, and Edward Jenner who discovered vaccination,

A view of the great hall, built in 1340, showing the dais

The long drawing-room

are among those who had cause to be grateful to the Berkeleys.

Situated on a mound by the Severn estuary and overlooking the extensive water meadows through which flows the Little Avon, the castle is a sombre yet glorious pile and, unlike so many places of its kind, is in an almost perfect state of preservation. It is, in fact, so complete as to afford an accurate insight into the defensive methods of bygone days without need of previous knowledge of ancient strongholds.

Whilst the history of the Manor of Berkeley goes back to the reign of Edward the Confessor, the actual castle was built as part of a defence system to keep the newly-won realm safe from the Welsh across the river. The man chosen by the Conqueror for the task of building and maintaining the system was William FitzOsbern, hereditary

steward of Normandy, and with Berkeley went also the responsibility for castles at Bristol, Hereford, Gloucester and Chepstow. Of the five, Berkeley is the only one which still remains complete.

Since those far-off days, there have been thirty-three owners of the castle and the various branches of the Berkeleys have intermarried with many of the great families of the land. Marriage ties have been contracted with the Earls of Derby, of March and of Surrey; the Dukes of Norfolk and Richmond, and a host more. To mention and identify even a tithe of the Berkeleys would require several volumes. There have been the very good and the very bad, and a whole lot in between. The appellation they received in their lifetime followed them into history, 'Make-peace', 'Magnanimous', 'Magnificent', 'Waste-all'—some now forgotten, some still standing out in high relief.

There was, for example, Thomas 'the Wise', who fought in the campaigns of Edward I and must have been a doughty warrior, for he fought at Bannockburn when seventy years of age, was made prisoner by the Scots, released on payment of ransom and lived on to the age of seventy-seven. His grandson, Thomas, was owner of the castle when that pitiable king, Edward II, was deposed by his wife and Roger Mortimer, Earl of March, and sent to end his days at Berkeley. Edward must have been tough, for he was subjected to many forms of torture, including sojourn in a dungeon where he was assailed by noxious vapours from decomposing cattle which would have meant certain death for others less hardy than Edward. Finally, two knights drove a red-hot rapier into his tortured body, using a cow's horn so that no trace of their crime would be visible. His screams are said to have reverberated round the dungeons and down even to the town beyond the castle walls. The king's body was kept for some months and eventually released to the Abbot of Gloucester, who gave him a martyr's tomb in the Cathedral. Thousands of pilgrims flocked to pay homage and it was the revenue so derived that made possible the rebuilding of part of the magnificent edifice we see today.

When Thomas Berkeley, the tenth Baron by tenure, died in 1417, he left no will and there were two claimants to the estate, his daughter, Elizabeth, wife of the Earl of Warwick, and a nephew, James Berkeley, who had been brought up in the castle as Thomas Berkeley's own son. After lengthy litigation, three manors were awarded to the Warwicks but eventually the Berkeleys seized the disputed ones. For a further fifty years the ownership continued in dispute until finally Elizabeth's grandson, Viscount Lisle, challenged Thomas Berkeley to a battle, the winner to take all, including the castle. Accepting the challenge, Thomas and his brothers assembled an army of a thousand men and, completely surprising their opponents by the size of the force mounted against them, put them to flight in the battle of Nibley Green.

Little detail is known of the battle but excavations in Nibley churchyard have disclosed a communal grave containing 150 skeletons. Viscount Lisle was killed and ownership of the disputed manors has lain with the Berkeleys ever since, except for a period when William, Marquess of Berk-

The portrait of Mary Cole, who was secretly married to the 5th Earl

eley, nicknamed 'Waste-all', bartered the castle with Henry VII and his heirs male, in pursuance of his insatiable desire for titles. Fortunately, after the death of Edward VI, the castle was restored to the family.

Under Henry VIII, a Berkeley served as royal standard-bearer and his cousin in the following century became Governor-General of Virginia. George, the ninth Baron, was created Earl of Berkeley by Charles II, while to John, a cousin of George, the monarch gave a plot of land, which eventually became Berkeley Square, in London. This was sold by the last Earl in the present century for some $2\frac{1}{2}$ million pounds, of which $1\frac{1}{2}$ million pounds were said to have been spent on restoring the castle.

During the Civil War of the seventeenth century, George Berkeley, the eighth Baron, owned the castle. Held for two years by the Royalists, it was put to siege and taken by the Cromwellians in

Van de Velde the elder's painting of HMS *Tyger*, commanded by a Berkeley

three days. The only lasting damage to the castle was a breach in the massive keep, made by mounting cannon on the roof of the nearby church and pounding away at short range. The breach has never been repaired.

The fifth Earl, Frederick Augustus, who died in 1810, fell in love with Mary Cole, a butcher's daughter and despite the Earl's assertions that they had been secretly married for some years, on his death the legitimacy of their son, William, born before their official marriage, was vehemently disputed. An interminable legal battle, which became known as the Berkeley Peerage case, ensued and was eventually referred to the House of Lords. William, in fact, did inherit the castle and was created Lord, and later Earl Fitzhardinge in his

own right. The eldest son of the official marriage inherited the Earldom of Berkeley but never claimed it.

One enters the castle today over a terrace which is flanked by trees growing where, in the fourteenth century, a moat surrounded the castle. The great shell keep with its gaping breach is to the left, beyond this there was formerly a draw-bridge and through the main fourteenth-century gateway the grooves on which the portcullis worked are still visible. The combination of tufa and the red sandstone of the Severn gives a pleasing hue to the outer walls, some of which are 14ft thick. To the left of the courtyard is a flight of worn stone steps leading through a twelfth-century doorway up to the keep, and the prison of Edward II. The dun-

22

The dining-room

geon is here 28ft in depth and goes down to courtyard level. Once lined with spikes, there is no exit from this deep well into which prisoners and the rotting carcases of animals were once pitched indiscriminately.

The medieval atmosphere of the castle has been so well preserved in the great kitchens that it is hard to believe they were in use up to 1942. They are adjacent to the courtyard, under which was the well, and all the ancient paraphernalia is still in place, including a gigantic spit some 10ft wide, huge and most unhygenic solid-lead sinks, enormous tiled game larders, pestle and mortar, chop-

ping blocks and many more contemporary items. Not of the fourteenth century is the cabinet containing forty bell signals, and the bells that were once used. The roof of these fascinating kitchens is magnificent, and the original timber first installed in the reign of Henry VII is still intact. An underground passage runs from the kitchens to the silver room, and the beer cellars, with eleven gigantic tuns, are a reminder of the days before the first world war when beer in enormous quantities was brewed on the estate.

The great hall, built in 1340, is 62ft long, 32ft wide and soars to a height of 32½ft. The superb fourteenth-century roof is contained within the twelfth-century curtain wall and little has been done to it since 1497. The screen at the end of the hall is sixteenth century and retains its original painted decoration. Over the dais hang two trophies, reminders of the history of this great family. One is the standard carried by the fourth Earl at the battle of Culloden Moor in 1746; the other, much smaller but even older, was captured on Flodden Field in 1513.

The morning-room was once the chapel, and again there is a wonderful timber roof. Little, unfortunately, remains of the painted decoration which contained verses from an early translation of the Bible made by a Cornishman, John Trevisa, who was chaplain at the castle in 1357 and a disciple of Wycliffe. A very fine fourteenth-century antiphonal, with square notes in the music, is believed to have been presented by the Pope to mark the consecration of the chapel. The king's pew, a fine screen balcony bearing the arms of Henry VII, was formerly in the chapel but has now been moved to the long drawing-room.

Beautiful tapestries adorn many of the castle rooms, and those in the morning-room comprise a series of early Brussels work illustrating the stories of Isaac and Rebecca, and Sodom and Gomorrah, woven by the Pannemakers after cartoons by

Raphael. The rich, red wall covering at the head of the grand staircase was, by tradition, part of the hangings of Henry VIII's pavilion at the Field of the Cloth of Gold. They have been in the castle since the seventeenth century.

Massive ship's timbers form the ceiling of the small drawing-room—of necessity, for immediately above this room the castle artillery was mounted. The required strength has been effectively married to an attractive appearance.

The dining-room, which once served as the guard-room, has the table laid for twelve with copies of a silver service which was the work of Jacques Roettiers, the French silversmith. The original service was sold at Sothebys ten years ago and realised the then unprecedented sum of £200,000. The portraits here include those of the twentieth-century owners of the castle, and most are wearing the yellow coats of the Berkeley Hunt. That of the present owner, is by John Teesdale, and was presented by the hunt committee. The last Earl's portrait is by Sir William Orpen.

The austere impression given by the castle from the outside is belied by the interior. The rooms are spacious, well-proportioned and light. Beautiful works of art abound, and the many pictures include family portraits by Hoppner, Wissing, Vermuyden, Battoni, Kneller, Lely, Zuccaro,

A venerable beam at the head of the grand staircase

The king's pew in the long drawing-room

Reynolds, Gainsborough, Cotes and many more. There are several works by Van de Velde, acknowledged the greatest of marine painters of the Dutch school. One picture depicting HMS *Tyger*, has pride of place, for this ship was commanded by a Berkeley, whose brother was an Admiral of the Blue. A picture by George Stubbs hangs in the picture gallery, with another of the Old Berkeley Hunt by Benjamin Marshall. Furniture and tapestries and china, exquisite embroidery and also a bedspread which is said to have belonged to Elizabeth I, are among the many other treasures.

The last Earl, the eighth, was a distinguished scientist and a Fellow of the Royal Society; twice married, he left no heir when he died in 1942. The Countess survives him and now lives in Italy. Captain R. G. W. Berkeley became the owner, and he died in 1969. The present owner is his son, Mr R. J. Berkeley, a lineal descendant in the twenty-fifth generation of Robert Fitzhardinge, who received the first grant of the castle in 1153. He has two sons, Charles and Henry.

Today the estate comprises some 6,000 acres, a far cry from the days when the Berkeley Hunt could ride from Gloucestershire to Charing Cross from centres owned by members of the family. Eventually the pack was divided, part to hunt in Berkeley country and the Old Berkeley to hunt the London country.

BLENHEIM PALACE

OXFORDSHIRE

Monument to a glorious age

The only palace in Britain which is neither royal nor episcopal. Blenheim stands in majesty in a park of 2,100 acres surrounded by delightful grounds and gardens and a vast expanse of lake, part natural, part artificial. The palace buildings alone cover three acres of ground and such is the symmetry of the state rooms that it is possible to close all the double doors dividing them and see the light at the far end through the keyholes, even though they follow one upon the other for more than a hundred yards. There are hundreds of chimneys, yet so ingenious is the architecture that hardly one is to be seen.

Superlatives are inseparable from Blenheim: its magnificent library is the largest in the country; the great ceremonial bronze gate weighs 17 tons; there is a bridge which is 35ft wide and an avenue of elms, said to be laid out in resemblance of the lines of opposing armies, which extends for 3,000 yards.

On this great and gracious monument to a bygone age was lavished the work of men of genius—Sir John Vanbrugh, Grinling Gibbons, Michael Rysbrack, Louis Laguerre, Sir James Thornhill,

The only palace in Britain that is neither royal nor episcopal

Part of the ceiling decoration in the saloon, painted by Louis Laguerre

'Capability' Brown and a host of others perhaps less well-known but equally gifted. Yet, strangely, the story surrounding this creation of so much that is beautiful is a dismal tale of intrigue and spite, hatred and viciousness, and long years of dissension in which few of those associated with the palace were not at times involved.

The manor of Woodstock was recorded in the Conqueror's Domesday Book as a royal forest, and in 1154 Henry II, who used the deer park, had his menagerie there. That illustrious young man, the Black Prince, was born in the manor, but not much disturbed its sleepy course until a grateful queen decided to honour her great captain. Then, over a period of twenty years, Blenheim Palace was built to become famous throughout the world in its own time, and a wonder to which future generations would come to marvel.

The story of the rise of John Churchill is well known; from a young page of honour to the Duke of York he became the greatest military commander of his age. He was by all accounts a handsome youth and after his marriage to Sarah Jennings, when she was eighteen, the couple went from strength to strength. She became first the friend and confidant of Queen Anne, and then a tyrant who ruled her royal mistress with a rod of iron. John Churchill (created Duke of Marlborough in 1689) went on to win a series of brilliant victories which settled the fate of Britain and Europe. Winston Churchill once wrote: 'Sarah managed the Queen and Marlborough managed the war, together with the smallest, most efficient executive that has ever ruled England.'

Marlborough's campaigns make exciting reading. When he took command, there were divided counsels among the allies and jealousy among the generals. Then, in 1704, came Blenheim, when

Ceiling of the green drawing-room designed by Hawksmoor

40,000 of the enemy were either killed, captured or wounded by the duke's armies. Campaign followed victorious campaign. In 1706, 40,000 horsemen were engaged by the opposing armies in a conflict which ended in the victory of Ramillies. Oudenarde followed in 1708, Malplaquet in 1709 and at long last, in 1712-13, the signing of the Treaty of Utrecht brought ten years of continuous victories to a triumphant conclusion and ended France's long domination of Europe. Little wonder that the nation, led by the queen, went wild with delight.

To honour her great general, Queen Anne bestowed upon him Woodstock Park, together with a grant towards the building of a house to be called Blenheim in memory of his most famous victory. Sir John Vanbrugh, fresh from his triumph at Castle Howard, was selected as architect. In February 1705, architect and duke met on the site and

the foundations were being dug within four months. Two years later, the east wing was ready for roofing. But things did not continue to run so smoothly. The duchess was antagonistic towards Vanbrugh, considering his plans to be extravagant, and the poor man must have suffered much. When Marlborough died in 1722 the mansion was still incomplete and at one period, when the Treasury was behind with payments, work stopped altogether. The final insult was when Vanbrugh took his wife to see the completed work and the duchess would not allow them in.

The actual completion gave rise to lawsuits and the final cost was £300,000, of which the duchess paid some £60,000. She could well afford it, for the joint emoluments the duke and duchess received from the state in their heyday totalled over £62,000 per annum, and on her death she left a fortune of three million pounds. After Marlborough's death, the duchess lived on for twenty-three years, embittered and friendless, quarrelling with everyone and everything except the memory of her husband, which she treasured and defended to the last. She was buried in the chapel at Blenheim and the body of the duke, which had lain in Westminster Abbey for twenty-two years, was brought by coach and six to lie beside her.

The buildings at Blenheim are arranged round three sides of an enormous courtyard, the central building containing four turrets and a portico supported by Corinthian columns. The wings, east and west, are joined by arcades forming courtyards, and the north and south fronts extend 350ft.

The main entrance leads into the great hall, soaring to a height of 67ft, where the magnificent ceiling by Thornhill at once captures the attention and a victorious Marlborough with the battle order at Blenheim unfolds. To the west (right) of the hall, and in striking contrast to almost everything else in the palace, is the contemporarily furnished room in which Sir Winston Churchill was born on 30 November 1874. Red-flowered paper covers the walls, there is a brass double bedstead and several mementoes of the great man, including some of his paintings.

The main staterooms run the length of the building and are divided by great mahogany double doors. Commencing from the east end, there is the green drawing-room with the original ceiling designed by Vanbrugh's collaborator, Nicholas Hawksmoor. The numerous portraits include a Romney of the fourth Duke and a Reynolds of the duchess. Others are by Lely and Kneller.

The red drawing-room has the wonderful Reynolds painting of the fourth Duke and Duchess and their family, a group of eight figures with three dogs, which is quite delightful. Here also is the fine painting of the ninth Duke and his family (1871-1934) by John Singer Sargent, the gifted American portrait painter. The green writing-room contains the most famous of the many tapestries, showing Marlborough accepting Marshal Tallard's surrender at Blenheim. Judocus de Vos, a weaver of Brussels, created the fantastic series which are to be seen in the staterooms. These depict victories won by the great duke and include those of Oudenarde and Malplaquet.

The adjoining room, formerly the saloon, is now used as the state dining-room. The painted walls

'The surrender at Blenheim', the finest of the tapestries

and ceiling are by Louis Laguerre, who was paid a fee of £500, and they are considered to be his best work. A Frenchman, he came to England in 1683 and worked for a time under Verrio (he succeeded Lely as Court Painter) at Christ's Hospital, London. One of the marble doorcases in the saloon is the work of Grinling Gibbons, who,

owing to a financial dispute, completed only the one.

From the saloon, the west wing accommodates another three staterooms, all of which are hung with the Blenheim tapestries. In every room beautiful paintings cover the walls and one of the most outstanding is that of Consuelo (*nee* Vanderbilt),

Rysbrack's elaborate memorial tribute to the Duke of Marlborough

ninth Duchess of Marlborough, by Carolus Duran.

The staterooms terminate with the long library which runs from north to south, a magnificent chamber originally designed as a picture gallery. Its purpose was changed to accommodate the Sunderland library, which was housed here until 1872, when it was sold. The ceiling with its two false domes is very fine and was the work of Isaac Mansfield. Paintings include full-length portraits of William III and Queen Anne by Kneller. At the southern end of the library is the statue of Queen Anne by Michael Rysbrack, which cost the duchess £300 and was a gracious gesture that 'all was forgiven'. The queen had by then been dead twenty-one years. Also in the library is a white marble bust of Marlborough.

At the northern end of the great room is the fine Henry Willis four-manual organ, which was installed by the eighth Duke in 1891. The front pipes are practically pure tin and on the grand occasion of its debut at Blenheim, Sir Arthur Sullivan was the organist. In 1931, a German firm installed a player mechanism manipulated by rolls, which at the time was unique for an instrument of this type.

The organ can now be played manually or mechanically. The inscription on the front of the organ reads:

> In memory of
> Happy Days
> and
> as a tribute to
> This Glorious Home
> We leave thy voice to speak
> within these walls
> in years to come
> when ours are still

The windows of the library look out on to the water terrace gardens.

The chapel at Blenheim was not finished until 1732, and is dominated by the great monuments in honour of the duke. His tomb was designed by William Kent and the work carried out by Rysbrack at a cost of £2,200. Considered the sculptor's finest work, it took him the best part of two years to complete.

The park with its lake extending over 131 acres provides a fitting setting for Blenheim. The gardens, laid out in the elaborate formal style which was the vogue in eighteenth-century France, were planned by Henry Wise, who was gardener to both

Queen Anne and George I. Adjacent to the long library, the ornamental scroll patterns of clipped box hedges are outlined in relief by coloured gravels, and statuary and fountains set them off to perfection.

The column of victory in the great avenue in the grounds is 134ft high and surmounted by a lead statue of the duke. On its base is recorded the battles in which he fought.

The main drive, 1½ miles long, is lined with elms which were planted at the turn of the century by the present duke's grandfather. It is regarded as the finest elm drive in Europe.

This great palace has been variously described. Horace Walpole called it 'a quarry of stone'; Sarah, in her anger, 'a wild and unmerciful house';

'We leave thy voice to speak within these walls'

Vanbrugh's bridge at Blenheim Palace

another critic saw it 'as massed battalions of stone like a declaration of war'. Conversely, it has been cited as a monument of the finest English baroque sculpture. Whatever else, it remains a monument to the generosity of a queen and the valour of a great soldier.

Today Blenheim is the example, par excellence, of how Britain's stately homes have become big business. In 1950, the number of visitors was 130,000; 1963, 110,00 and then in 1965, 220,000. By 1972 this figure had risen to 260,100.

Half-a-mile across the park from Blenheim, the little churchyard at Bladon contains the grave of that famous kinsman of the duke, Sir Winston Churchill, who will equally be remembered as a saviour of his country. A man with a strong sense of family loyalty, he made it clear long before his death that he wished to lie with his parents close to his birthplace. There he was buried and nearby now lies his son, Randolph, who died in 1968. Thousands have made the pilgrimage to Sir Winston's grave and each year the numbers grow.

BROUGHTON CASTLE
OXFORDSHIRE

Historic stronghold of the Civil War

Broughton Castle is a superb example of beauty combined with medieval splendour. Little has altered in this peaceful corner of the Oxfordshire countryside in the seven hundred years since the castle was built, and though its wide encircling moat is today carpeted with water lilies there were times in its long history, particularly during the Civil War of the seventeenth century, when it was used to grim purpose.

Broughton had its origins in a medieval manor house built about 1300 by Sir John de Broughton, who owned the manor of that name. Sir John also built the church, which stands a stone's throw from the present gatehouse. A span of fifty years of occupation by the family followed, and then, in 1377, the house passed into the hands of that great Englishman, William of Wykeham, the churchman and statesman who became Bishop of Winchester and over a period of twenty-five years was twice Chancellor of the realm. He also founded New College, Oxford, and Winchester School.

His heir, Sir Thomas Wykeham, obtained a licence to convert the manor house into a fortified castle, and as such it was subsequently inherited

Floodlighting emphasises the simple dignity of the Castle

A bridge spans the moat and leads to the
fourteenth-century gatehouse

by Sir Thomas's granddaughter, Margaret. On her
marriage in 1451 to Sir William Fiennes, second
Lord Saye and Sele, it passed into the ownership
of that family, in whose hands it has remained
ever since.

Few alterations were made for the next one hundred years then, in Elizabethan times, Richard
Fiennes decided to enlarge and modernise the
castle. He took out the roof of the great hall, added
two storeys with two large rooms at the west end,
and two staircases on the south side. The work
was eventually completed by his son, Richard, in
1599, leaving it as we see it today.

The Civil War brought exciting times to the

owner had been created a viscount by James I in
1624, but his strong puritanical leanings led him
naturally to become a Parliamentarian when fric-
tion developed between King and Parliament. In a
secret room in the castle many of the men who
were to become prominent Cromwellians met to
discuss their plans. They included John Pym, John
Hampden, Sir Henry Vane, Sir John Eliot and
William, Lord Saye and Sele, who it was said by
his detractors: 'Had the deepest hand in all the
evils that befell the unhappy kingdom.'

When the war broke out Lord Saye and Sele and
his four sons were soon involved in the fighting in
the Midlands, and in 1642 their regiment of blue-

night before Edgehill, the battle in which Oliver Cromwell made his mark as a captain of horse. The castle fell to the superior forces of the Royalists without a fight and Prince Rupert and his men pillaged the place. Later, with the changing fortune of the war, it was laid to siege and retaken by the Roundheads. When the war was over, Lord Saye and Sele refused to be associated with the execution of Charles I, or even to sit in Cromwell's House of Lords. Instead, he prudently retired to Lundy Island, in the Bristol Channel,

Known as 'Old Subtlety', this William had earned the nickname by his cunning as a parliamentary tactician and his astuteness in council. A brilliant politician, with the courage of his convictions, he was also wise enough when the Restoration drew near, to hasten to assure Charles II of his loyalty. He was pardoned and appointed Lord Privy Seal in 1660. He died at Broughton and is buried in the church there.

His son, Nathaniel, remained an unrepentant Puritan. He became speaker of Cromwell's House of Lords and was one of the committee which strongly urged Cromwell to accept the crown. It was Nathaniel's daughter, Celia, who, towards the end of the seventeenth century, made journeys all over England and wrote vigorous accounts of the life and habits of the ordinary people.

The fourteenth Baron's one claim to fame was that he was the oldest peer in the House of Lords,

The interior of the great hall

and it was his son, William Thomas (later the fifteenth Baron) who was a member of the Prince Regent's set. His indulgence in all the excesses that were then popular, including pugilism, cock-fighting and horse-racing, must have drained the family fortunes, for in his time there was a great sale at which all the pictures, furniture and other works of art in the castle were sold. He survived his father by only three years, dying at the early age of forty-seven.

Of the original manor house built by John de Broughton a considerable part survives, including the crypt which was under the chapel, and the stairs which William of Wykeham installed in

The long gallery

1380, leading off the superb groined passage built about 1300.

Easily discernible on the west front are the windows which were filled in during the alterations of 1554. High up in the walls, they are an indication of the height of the medieval hall. Today the main entrance is here and the great hall occupies the central position, covering an area 54ft long by 30ft wide. Of the many interesting items on display, not least are the array of leather fire buckets, bearing the family crest, a Parliamentarian trooper's leather coat, and the bag bearing the cypher of Charles I in which 'Old Subtlety' used to carry the Privy Seal.

One of the finest rooms in the castle is the oak drawing-room with its elaborately carved interior porch. The room is panelled in oak from floor to ceiling and the whole was painted white in 1660 by 'Old Subtlety' as a mark of his delight in the restoration. The motto in Latin over the porch is freely translated as: 'What once was, gives me least pleasure to remember'—presumably the heartfelt sentiments of the old man. The panelling has since been cleaned and brought back to its original natural state. Over the chimneypiece is a seascape by Joannes Peeters, depicting Charles II setting sail from Holland for his return to England. The dining-room has a fourteenth-century vaulted roof, and some very handsome early sixteenth-century double linen-fold panelling.

Part of the enlargement of the castle in 1554 was the installation of the main staircase. At a turn in the stairs on the second storey there is a small low-ceilinged room, where almost certainly the servants and aides of the Puritan leaders waited while their masters plotted in the room immediately above. To pass the time, they amused themselves by signing their names on the plaster ceiling in candle smoke, and traces of this are still discernable.

The room above, known as the council chamber, has the sombre atmosphere befitting its history, and it is easy to imagine the Puritan lords, Hampden, Pym and others, meeting to lay their plans, well guarded by their henchmen below.

Pictures on the stairway include portraits of some of the prominent men of those days. One is of William Prynne, the rabid Puritan who was always in trouble. Years before the Civil War he cast aspersions on the queen's character and, as a result, was fined £5,000 and had his ears lopped off. A strange man, he hated independence equally with episcopacy, and was an indefatigable writer of tracts upon the many and varied subjects upon which he held strong opinions. He exhausted his vocabulary and men's patience by attacking all and sundry. First the queen, then the king and, in due course, the Parliamentarians suffered his abuse. When he was branded on both cheeks with the letters 'SL' (seditious libeller), he shouted to by-standers: 'The more I am beat down, the more I am lift up.' An accurate prophecy as it proved, for, like 'Old Subtlety', he came into his own at the Restoration with important state positions and a pension of £500 a year.

The long gallery abounds with family portraits, including a fine Gainsborough of the wife of the thirteenth Lord Saye and Sele and a portrait of the fifteenth Baron, who was a notorious gambler.

One of the bedrooms off the gallery, known as the star chamber, has late eigthteeenth-century Chinese hand-painted wallpaper, which looks as fresh as if it had only recently been produced. In this room James I slept when he visited Broughton a year after he had ascended the throne. At the end of the gallery is the queen's room, where Queen Anne of Denmark slept during a visit. Here a pair of small folding doors affords a view down to the fourteenth-century private chapel In later days, Edward VII used this same room on the many occasions when he visited Broughton, one of the attractions being that it was a convenient place for meeting with Lady 'Darling Daisy' Warwick, meetings which eventually led to a considerable scandal. A door at a corner of this gallery gives on to the original turret stairs which have a most unusual stone handrail.

The roof, access to which is near the attic where the troopers slept before the battle of Edgehill, is the ideal vantage point from which to view the surroundings. Immediately below is the formal garden and beyond, the moat fed by the Sor brook, and a wide vista over the beautiful Oxfordshire countryside. The gatehouse, and the church with its graceful fourteenth-century tower crowned by a spire, are grouped close by.

When the television series 'The Six Wives of Henry VIII' was being made, Broughton Castle proved the perfect setting for the filming of the Jane Seymour episodes, its authenticity removing

The attractive and well-kept
formal garden

all need for props. More recently—in 1971, a *Son et Lumiere* at the castle, a well-staged amateur effort by the Lions Club of Banbury, proved a great success. The present owner of the castle is the twenty-first Lord Saye and Sele to hold the title. He served in the Greenjackets in the last war and took part in the Normandy landings. Lord and Lady Saye and Sele have four children, three boys and a girl.

WILLIAM THOMAS
12ᵀᴴ LORD SAYE AND SE

One of the many family portraits—the 12th Lord Saye and Sele

CHASTLETON HOUSE

GLOUCESTERSHIRE

A Jacobean mansion of character

Chastleton House stands where four of England's most beautiful counties meet. The borders of Gloucestershire, Worcestershire, Warwickshire, and Oxfordshire converge within half-a-mile of the house which, from its height of 600ft above sea level, affords wonderful views over many miles of the countryside. The house is typically early seventeenth century, as is the group formed by the mansion, the church and the stone dovecot—a fair illustration of a style characteristic of this region of England.

The estate once belonged to that strange, stormy petrel, Robert Catesby, who inherited it from his grandmother, one of the famous Warwickshire family of Throckmorton. Nothing is known about the house or the estate of that time, except that it must have been of considerable extent. The young man was a recusant before he

The two corner towers accommodate the staircases

The long gallery, with its magnificent coved plasterwork ceiling

went to Oxford and undoubtedly the harsh treatment suffered by his father for his faith had some influence on young Robert, leading possibly to his participation in the Earl of Essex's ill-fated rebellion of 1601. Catesby was one of his prominent adherents and when the rising was crushed and the Earl of Essex beheaded, Catesby was pardoned for his part but fined 4,000 marks (probably some £35,000 by today's values) and so was forced to sell the Chastleton estate. Later the unfortunate young man was deeply involved in the Gunpowder Plot and was killed while resisting arrest.

The estate, which then comprised perhaps 1,000 acres or more, was sold in 1603 to Walter Jones, a wool-stapler and Member of Parliament for Worcester, who very soon began to build the great and gracious house which now stands virtually unaltered from the original plan. The exact date of completion is uncertain, though it is known that

the work was in progress in 1609 when Henry, his son, contracted what was obviously an advantageous marriage with Anne Fettiplace, judging by a jingle of those days which ran:

The Lacy's, the Tracy's and the Fettiplace's
They own all the parks, the manors and the chases.

The couple eventually settled down at Chastleton and established a role for the family as country gentlefolk which was to last until the end of the eighteenth century.

There were exciting events during the civil wars. Arthur Jones, who owned Chastleton in 1651 when Charles II was defeated at Worcester, escaped from the field of battle and made his way to Chastleton, closely pursued by Parliamentary troopers. He arrived in time to be spirited away to a secret room which opened off one of the bedrooms, but his weary horse in the stables betrayed his presence. His enemies searched the house and finding nothing, but still suspicious, decided to stay the night in the bedroom overlooking the stables. Unfortunately, the secret hideout opened off the same room. The fugitive's resourceful wife Sara, however, fed the troopers and, it is suspected, drugged their supper beer with opium from her medicine chest, so that she was able to lead her husband over their sleeping forms to the stables. There he took the troop commander's horse and made good his escape, eventually to France. Happily husband and wife were reunited at Chastleton in time to welcome the Restoration, but unrecompensed by a grateful sovereign, the heavy fine they had sustained because of their Royalist sympathies kept them and their descendants poor.

Towards the end of the eighteenth century, two brothers, John and Arthur Jones, lived at Chastleton but neither had any offspring to inherit the estate. A chance meeting with a remote cousin at Chipping Norton Mop Fair, resulted in that cousin's son inheriting the estate on the death of the two brothers in 1828. The new owner was John Henry Whitmore, who added the name and arms of Jones to his own and became Whitmore Jones. Seven years before he came into the property he had married Dorothy Clutton who, in the course of time, presented her husband with a family of four boys and six girls. After their father's death, three of the sons inherited Chastleton in turn.

Five of the six girls of the family married and by an odd coincidence four married clergymen, three of whom were brothers. On the death of her brothers, Mary, the only unmarried daughter, came into the property and she is best remembered as having been a ferocious Tory.

Mary's father had been improvident, if not reckless, and in the seventies, with the importation

Features of the great chamber are the panelling, and the coloured plaques of prophets and sybils

of cheap corn from America and the great agricultural slump, life became so difficult that she had to let the house. She kept the estate intact, however, and when a nephew, Thomas, inherited, he became Thomas Whitmore Jones. He managed the estate well enough until he died, when his wife sold most of it. She returned to the house to live just before the second world war and the present owner, Mr Alan Clutton-Brock, came into posession in 1955.

It would seem that none of the families who lived in the house was particularly wealthy and perhaps this has been a blessing in disguise, for scarcely any alterations have been made to the original building plan in the course of more than three centuries. The impression gained of this Jacobean mansion from the outside is of a gracious and stately home of character, which indeed it is for it has always been lived in. The soaring gables and the two fine corner towers which accommodate the staircases give the place a solid yet far from ponderous appearance.

Inside, the medieval plan is followed with the great hall opening off the screens passage, which passes from front to rear of the building. The screen (and indeed most of the woodwork throughout the house) is of oak. Handsomely carved, it is topped by obelisks, known as pyramids, which are also prominent in the masonry surmounting the main door, on the facade, in carvings and even adorning the top of the stairway well.

The hall has an eight-light oriel and a dais for the high table. Portraits of members of the various families associated with Chastleton are numerous, and in the hall Arthur Jones, the Cavalier, is portrayed, though from the portrait he looks anything but a hunted fugitive. A queer conceit is a huge pair of caribou antlers which an eighteenth-century

The great parlour, rich with plaster ceiling and tapestries

A window in the great chamber parlour contains portraits of Charles I and his queen

owner must have felt looked rather lonely, so he had painted on the wall a sadly out-of-proportion animal to go with them.

There are three parlours on the ground floor, two of which open out of the great hall. The white parlour is panelled in oak from floor to ceiling but, unfortunately, it has all been painted white.

In the great parlour, a fine room with a superb plaster ceiling, a seventeenth-century Flemish tapestry almost covers one wall. It depicts the gay scene of a return from the hunt, the huntsmen enjoying refreshment in a formal garden while the peasants dance to a tune played by village musicians.

There are two stairways, the 'best' stairs and the back stairs, the latter being unusual in that the well is entirely enclosed and large cupboards, each with finely-wrought decorative iron hinges, have been built in at every landing. At the top, the well has been covered over and pyramids decorate each corner.

The principal bedroom of the house is hung with

tapestries which are noted in an inventory of 1633. It is obvious that the panelling was specially made to fit and finish the room, which itself must have been planned in the first place to accommodate the tapestries. Older than the house, they were brought from Worcestershire and their design depicts the story of Jacob and Esau. The attractive plaster frieze is Jacobean and the oak overmantel, carved in 1609, bears the Fettiplace arms and quarterings.

On the first floor is the great chamber where in earlier days all business was transacted. The panelling from floor to ceiling is most beautifully carved. Almost at ceiling height are a series of twenty-four coloured plaques which extend round two sides of the room. They comprise twelve Jacobean paintings of Old Testament prophets and twelve Sibyls. Recently restored, their elegance brings a touch of lightness to the panelling. The family arms are on the stone chimneypiece.

The middle chamber, formerly a bedroom, has been modernised and on display there is a Worcester tea service, each piece carrying the arms of the Jones family. Here, too, are portraits by Thomas Hudson of Thomas Clutton and Annaretta, his wife.

Another of the main bedrooms is the one in which the Parliamentary troopers spent the night. The secret room is in a corner and it is assumed that in those exciting days it was disguised as a cupboard, a false back sliding open to give access to the hide-out. Its present window is obviously a later addition. The four-poster bed is impressive, but it is the bedspread that catches the eye for its very beautiful and intricate Florentine work. Not surprisingly, it took the wife of Walter Jones (circa 1680) fifteen years to stitch it.

The well-stocked library contains many fine eighteenth-century editions but was obviously not meant to be used in the winter, for it has no fireplace.

The greatest glory of Chastleton is undoubtedly the long gallery, which is 72ft long by 18ft wide The coved plasterwork ceiling is magnificent and is believed to have been the work of travelling craftsmen who carried with them moulds of various designs from which the client could choose, much as one might choose wallpaper today.

All about the house are objects of interest. There is an exercise horse, sometimes called a chamber horse, which consists of a padded seat supported by powerful springs. Housebound in bad weather, people could at least obtain some exercise by sitting on it and working the springs up and down There is a pillion saddle, a slipper bath shaped like a gigantic shoe, and a hobby horse which no doubt gave the children of an earlier period much enjoyment.

There are also many historic treasures, two of which are closely associated with Charles I. On the scaffold, the monarch gave his Bible to Bishop Juxon, his chaplain, and as a treasured relic it was handed down to members of the bishop's family With the death of his last descendant in the eighteenth century, it was given to the Squire of Chastleton, Henry Jones, possibly because the family was known for its strong Jacobite sympathies, and is still treasured at Chastleton today.

The other and quite fascinating reminder of the monarch is a miniature of Charles I painted on copper. With it are a set of sixteen transparencies painted on mica and each, when fitted over the master, shows a different posture. Thus depicted

are the king with crown and sceptre; as a prisoner at Carisbrooke; being presented with the warrant for his execution; with Bishop Juxon reading the Bible; the executioner binding the king's eyes; the executioner lifting the decapitated head; and the head with the martyr's laurel crown. This treasure is one of only four sets which were made for Henrietta Maria, queen of Charles I.

The garden of Chastleton includes a box garden surrounded by a yew hedge which, through the years, has become a triumph of topiary art. It dates from 1690-1700, when elaborate topiary

A ship under sail—one of many fine examples of topiary work

work first became the fashion, and generations of gardeners have since tended the yews with skill and devotion to produce the twenty-four shapes which delight the eye today. Dogs, rabbits, a bear, a ship in sail, all grown as was the practice on wire or metal frameworks, are but a few and in 1952 a crown was created in honour of the coronation of Queen Elizabeth II.

In the park opposite the great house there is a massive and ancient stone dovecote which belonged not to Chastleton but to a house which stood close to the dovecote. To gain some privacy, the owners of the house built a great wall and as Chastleton rose, storey by storey, so their wall grew higher and higher. It must have been a monstrous sight. No records survive about this second house but the wall was eventually demolished and the land on which it stood reverted to the owners of Chastleton.

COMPTON WYNYATES

WARWICKSHIRE

A Tudor treasure

The warm glow of red brick, a forest of chimneys nestling deep in a great hollow and the glint of moat and fishpond in the sunshine—these are the first, and indeed lasting, impressions of this Tudor house which lies just over the Warwickshire border from both Oxfordshire and Gloucestershire. Set in unspoiled countryside and unusually remote in being some two and a half miles from the nearest village, Compton Wynyates is surrounded but not overshadowed by wooded hills on which the trees rise up in tiers on three sides and only to the north is there a 'wind gate' with a windmill which was working in living memory silhouetted against the hillside.

The strawberry-hued bricks of which the house is built were made close by and have weathered the centuries as only the products of the old craftsmen seem to do. The twisted chimneys, and there are forty of them, rise at odd places, the gables are of unequal height and uneven pitch and, like the turrets of different shapes, all add their quota to the charm of this magnificent building.

The layout of the house appears to be very irregular at first sight but, once inside, it becomes obvious that the hardcore of the plan is a square around a courtyard. Other extensions have been made through the centuries but they have in no way detracted from what is essentially a sensible and practical building.

This quiet corner of Warwickshire has been a home of the Compton family since the thirteenth century, when Philip de Compton was lord of the manor. He was succeeded by other descendants, all of whom were important men in the county. It was Edmund who married an heiress and towards the end of the fifteenth century built the present house on the site of an earlier manor house. It then comprised the four wings round a quadrangle and his work is easily discerned by the stone-slated roofs and the walls—4ft thick.

When Edmund died his eleven-year-old son, William, became a ward of the Court and was appointed page to Henry VII's son, Henry, then aged two. It was an appointment which was to have lasting and fortunate results for the Compton family. When the prince, through the death of his brother, ascended the throne as Henry VIII, William became first gentleman of the bedchamber and a constant companion and favourite of the king. Honours were heaped upon him up to the time of his death, including the unusual permission to wear his hat in the king's presence and, later, the unique privilege of augmenting his coat-of-arms with the royal lion of England. The document licensing this grant hangs in the dining-room to this day.

William Compton was at the king's side when the military expedition left for France in 1512, and after the victory at Tournai he was knighted for gallantry in the field.

Among the gifts he received was Fulbroke Castle, near Warwick. True it was in a ruinous state but the materials came in useful to embellish Compton Wynyates. The timber ceiling in the great hall and the lovely bay window which projects into the courtyard are among the items which were so fortunately salvaged.

Sir William, who had so firmly established the family fortunes, died in 1528 from sweating sickness, leaving an only son, Peter, who at six years of age became a ward of Cardinal Wolsey. He died, however, a minor, but leaving a son who was created Baron Compton by Queen Elizabeth and whose son was made Earl of Northampton by King James I. Spencer, second Earl of Northampton, was a godson of Queen Elizabeth and during the reign of James I became a favourite of the prince who was to become Charles I.

It was during the lifetime of the second Earl that the Civil War between the King and Parliament took place and the Comptons, ever loyal to the king, played a notable part in the troubles. One of the nine lords impeached by Parliament, Spencer raised a troop of 100 gentlemen and took to the field. Later he raised a regiment of horse, command of which was given to his eldest son. With three of his six sons he fought at the battle of Edgehill only six miles from the house, and it is recorded that his fourth son, then aged thirteen, was indignant at not being allowed to share the dangers with his brothers, though he did later. Their father, however, was killed at the battle of Hopton Heath in 1643.

The close proximity of the fighting, combined with the deep involvement of the family, made Compton Wynyates a certain target for the Parliamentarians. In 1644 they laid seige to the house, which was only able to withstand the assault for two days. The earl's widow and younger son were captured, the church was destroyed and its monuments were thrown into the moat. All the deer in the park were slaughtered and the Parliamentary troops took 120 prisoners, £5,000 in money (some of which was found in earthenware pots buried in the moat), sixty horses, 400 sheep, cattle and eighteen loads of other plunder. The story goes that the widowed mother of the second Earl remained in the house whilst it was garrisoned to tend the wounded Cavaliers who were concealed in hiding-places in the roof.

After the war, a fine of £20,000 was imposed on the family and orders were given to fill in the moat and destroy the battlements. The estates were confiscated but eventually they were handed back to the family.

When Charles II regained the throne Henry Compton, the sixth son, served in the Royal Horse Guards, but later he took Holy Orders and eventually became Bishop of London and an ardent supporter of the Protestant cause. He was signatory to the invitation extended to William of Orange to accept the crown.

A devastation different to that of the Civil War befell Compton Wynyates in 1768, when the family was temporarily ruined by one of the most remarkable elections ever to take place in English history. Because of the enormous expenditure of money it involved, it became known as the 'Spend-

The main entrance, surmounted by the royal arms

thrift' election. The fight for two Parliamentary seats for the borough of Northampton had little or no concern with politics but was entirely a personal contest between, not the candidates, but three Northamptonshire peers who each supported a different candidate. Lord Northampton nominated his brother-in-law, Admiral Sir George Rodney; Lord Halifax, Sir George Osborne his nephew; and Lord Spencer, his neighbour Sir James Langham, who subsequently withdrew. Rodney and

47

Osborne were both Tories, Langham was a Whig, and bribery and corruption were rife in both parties.

The election is estimated to have cost Lord Spencer £100,000, and Lord Northampton and Lord Halifax £150,000. Lord Halifax was ruined and had to sell his house and estate. Lord Northampton, to meet his liabilities, cut down all the trees on his Castle Ashby estate to the value of £50,000 and sold all the furniture of Compton Wynyates and much from Castle Ashby. The castle was then closed and Northampton left the country to spend the rest of his life in a modest villa in Switzerland. He had also given orders for Compton Wynyates to be demolished but, fortunately for posterity, his agent found a variety of excuses for delay and it was saved. It lay derelict until about 1835 when the second Marquess had some much-needed repairs made to it. His son furthered the work but fifty years were to pass until the fifth Marquess came to occupy it. The present and sixth Marquess has installed heating and electric light and added considerably to the furnishings of the house.

Approaching the house, it is at once obvious that it was built in this very secluded place with an eye to defence and the availablity of water with which to fill the moat. Outlined in concrete in front of the main entrance is the position of the pier of the stone bridge and the causeway on to which the drawbridge was lowered. Carved in the stone of the porch are the arms of Henry VII and Henry VIII, and round it in Latin a dedication: *My Lord King Henry 8th*. In the spandrels of the arch are Tudor badges.

Inside the arch are two notches worn by the chains of the inner drawbridge, and from these positions diminutive side doors gave access to boats on the moat when the drawbridge was up. To the left is the original guardroom.

Once through the outer gateway, the visitor finds an attractive courtyard, 57ft square, on the far side of which is the main door which, in turn, leads by way of nineteenth-century doors in the screen

The south front. The oriel window lights the chapel

to the great hall. The screen dates from the time of Henry VIII, though some of the carved panels are even older. One, beautifully carved, depicts French and English knights in battle at Tournai, the detail of the horses being particularly fine. Above the screen is the minstrel gallery and higher still the superb original Henry VII timbered ceiling. The walls of the great hall are rich with linenfold panelling, and here everyone, lord and retainers, ate in company. One of the long tables they used still remains; of elm, it is 23ft long, 28in wide and 3in thick. A graceful bay window at the southern end of the hall and facing on to the courtyard is believed to have come from Fulbroke Castle and has been very skilfully fitted into its present position. The louvre through which the smoke from the fire in the centre of the hall once escaped, is still retained.

The dining-room was partitioned in 1512 to form an ante-chapel when the chapel was added, and the beautifully-panelled drawing-room on the first floor is enriched by a plaster ceiling which dates from the Elizabethan period.

The most notable of the rooms after the great hall, however, is Henry VIII's room, so-called because the monarch who did so much for the Comptons occupied it on the occasions of his several visits. The glass of the windows displays the arms of Henry and Catherine of Aragon, other coats of arms and the Tudor rose. The panelling dates from about 1630, as does the ceiling which carries the royal monograms of four monarchs who are known to have stayed in the house: Henry VIII, Elizabeth I, James I and Charles I. The gold bed used by them was pillaged by the Roundhead commander, but was recovered much later by the third Earl and returned to Compton Wynyates. Unfortunately, it was sold during the family's financial crisis in the eighteenth century, when it realised only £10.

The chapel contains some curious carvings and an organ made by the famous Father Smith. All the Wren churches in London after the Great Fire contained organs made by Smith. This instrument, which has a beautiful tone, was so designed that the organist had to stand to play it and the

The east front. Note the array of chimneys

keyboard notes which are normally black, are white, and vice versa. An oil painting on the communion table, representing Christ carrying the Cross, is attributed to Cristoforo Caselli (1488-1521).

Compton Wynyates has a host of secret rooms, doors, passages and hidey-holes which must have been put to good use in its more exciting days—and not least, perhaps, the secret door which leads from the royal bedroom to a passage. A dressing-room adjoining, and off the passage, has a small turret stair no more than 30in wide.

The council chamber is remarkable in having six doors opening from it. There were three small staircases which led to the room above, whilst three more descended to the room below. The panelling

The door on to the courtyard from the buttery and kitchens, the oldest part of the house. Three of the dormer windows of the 'barracks' can be seen

The oriel in the hall which was
brought from Fulbroke Castle

The Elizabethan drawing-room

of the chamber is unusual in being tongued and grooved so that each piece fits tightly together and presents a smooth surface on which plaster or decorative painting could be applied. Fortunately, nothing was ever added and the oak has been left in its natural state, the graining presenting a most pleasing appearance.

It is said that sometime in the fascinating history of Compton Wynyates, a priest was hidden in the house and one room he is reputed to have used certainly has all the necessary requirements. An oak plank which lies against the window bears crudely carved crosses to support the theory that it was used as an altar, and there are five escape routes from the room, three of them by way of small turret stairways.

Long ago Compton children playing in another room noted a hollow sound from part of the wall and persuaded their parents to investigate. It was then that the room known as the Cavaliers' room was discovered. Here again there is a turret stair-

way but differing from the others in that the steps are of the red brick of which the house is built. Whatever their purpose, the very worn state of the stairs shows that they were put to considerable use. Tiny slit windows in the room face three ways, so that it could have been an excellent lookout post, and perhaps it was here that the wounded Cavaliers were hidden by the mother of the second Earl.

An interesting feature in the chapel drawing-room, from which services in the chapel below could be watched, were the open mullions. Only comparatively recently have they been glazed. The stone fireplace is the original and must have given considerable comfort to those seated in such a draughty position.

Perhaps most fascinating of all in this amazing house is the section known as the 'barracks', which merges with the roof. A number of dormer windows give light and it is said to have been the quarters of 400 royal troopers in the Civil War period. Originally, it ran unbroken along the whole length of the south wing of the courtyard. At a later date it was divided into ten sections comprising a dozen or more rooms, the divisions being dictated by massive oak beams which lie on the floor, across the width. Obviously capable of accommodating a great many men in its original plan, the 'barracks' are still most impressive in their present form.

Every room in Compton Wynyates has fine furniture, interesting objects, paintings and other works of art. In the hall a painting by Marco Palmezzano of Forli depicts the mystic marriage of St Catherine, and was originally painted as an altar piece for an Italian church. Here, too, is a tapestry of the sixteenth century, thought to have been designed by Giulio Romano, a distinguished pupil of Raphael. The portraits of the seven Comptons who took part in the Civil War adorn the dining-room and, at the foot of the main staircase, there are very fine portraits of the present

Marquess and his lady, painted by Alice M. Burton in 1964.

Drawing-room treasures include a rare piece of sixteenth-century embroidery which was worked over a mould and known as stump work, and a picture by the Venetian artist, Giorgione, which is remarkable for the freshness of its colours after nearly 500 years. A pastoral scene, it was exhibited in Venice in 1955. There is also a very fine painting of the Crucifixion by Matteo Balducci.

On the wall of the council chamber hangs a panel of Sheldon tapestry made in the neighbouring village of Barcheston. In the sixteenth century Squire Sheldon gave employment to some Flemish weavers and so produced the first tapestries made in England.

At Castle Ashby, the Compton's home near Northampton, there were in the seventeenth century eighty-seven house servants and eighteen gardeners. Compton Wynyates, while not aspiring to

The entrance front to Compton Wynyates

quite such grandeur, also had a large staff to which the site of the old kitchens bears witness. Great oak beams span the ceilings, and the folding doors leading from the buttery to the kitchens are decorated with linenfold panelling and fitted with a cleverly contrived folding piece, which could be set up as a temporary table. A large metal-lined ice box served as a refrigerator and in one corner there is a very large game larder. There are also a variety of mechanical roasting jacks and a curious enclosure, or pen, which is said to have housed a live sheep. Close by were the dungeons, now put to a more peaceful purpose.

On the south side of the house lies a garden of walks surrounded by clipped yews and, farther over, a pond which drains through to what remains of the moat. On the eastern side a formal garden flanks the moat, now covered with giant water lilies, and beyond are fish ponds which in their time provided the household with food.

This lovely house may have been built for defensive purposes, but it has none of the atmosphere usually associated with a fortified building. Peace pervades the whole scene and the house is essentially a family home. Perhaps it is fortunate that for so long it was not the principal home of the family and so was spared, the excessive restoration and modernisation dictated by changing fashions through the centuries.

The present Marquess (sixth) succeeded to the title in 1913 and he and Lady Northampton spend some months of each year at Compton Wynyates. He served in the 1914-18 War, in which he was wounded, twice mentioned in despatches and awarded the DSO. He commanded the Warwickshire Yeomanry in 1933, and served as chairman of the Northants County Council until resigning in 1955. There are two sons and two daughters.

The church which was destroyed when the Parliamentary forces captured the house was rebuilt in 1665, and several figures which, after mutilation, had been thrown into the moat, were recovered and restored to their positions. The pews and altar rails are *circa* 1720.

The church's close association with the Compton family is evident throughout. On display are banners which were carried in the Civil War, hatchments of the family, and the Garter Knight's banner and helmet crest which hung in St George's Chapel at Windsor during the fifth Marquess's lifetime.

On the south aisle a tablet to the memory of the fifth Marquess notes that he was the first of the family since 1768 to make Compton Wynyates his home. On the north aisle there is a reminder that the family have carried their loyal tradition into the twentieth century. Displayed there is the sword carried by Lord Spencer Compton, a lieutenant in the Royal Horse Guards, killed in action at Ypres on 13 May, 1915.

DITCHLEY

OXFORDSHIRE

A lovely eighteenth-century mansion

Ditchley, one of the finest of the eighteenth-century mansions of Oxfordshire, lies close to the town of Charlbury. There has been an estate and a house on the site site close by the village of Spelsbury probably from the thirteenth century, and Sir Henry Lee purchased the estate, and presumably a house, in 1583. Coming from Quarrendon, near Aylesbury, he decided to live at Ditchley when he was appointed Ranger of the Royal Forest of Woodstock and Knight of the Garter, by Elizabeth I.

Nothing remains of this earlier Tudor house, though it was obviously sumptuous enough for the entertainment of royalty, since Elizabeth I and several of the Stuart kings were guests there. Some souvenirs of their visits have, however, survived and in the saloon of the present house are the antlers of six red deer killed by a royal hunting

The north-east frontage of Ditchley. The house cost £9,000 to build in 1772

One of the beautiful hall
doorways, the work of
William Kent

party, each bearing a plate engraved with the details.

Sir Henry died without a male heir and the estate was inherited by a relative, another Henry, who was the eldest of eight sons. He was the first Baronet and died in 1631, after which his widow married three more husbands, each an earl. The son of her first husband succeeded and when he died his widow married the Earl of Rochester. Their only son became the notorious rake of Restoration days. Lady Rochester continued to live at Ditchley after her second marriage and the estate was miraculously kept intact throughout the Civil War.

One of the intrepid lady's grandsons, Sir Edward Henry Lee, married Charlotte Fitzroy, daughter of Charles II and his notorious mistress Barbara Villiers, who was to become Duchess of Cleveland. The couple were aged fourteen and twelve at the time of the marriage, but it had its compensations for not only were there eighteen children of the marriage (thirteen of them sons), but the youthful husband was created first Earl of Litchfield, Viscount Quarrendon and Baron of Spelsbury. Charlotte's many years of childbearing apparently still left her time to develop her domestic talents, for she left a book in nearby Spelsbury church containing over 300 recipes. A memorial tablet recording the deaths of these two recalls their marriage in the extravagant language of the day. They were, it states: 'the most gallant bridegroom and most beautiful bride of the court.'

The sixth son of this union succeeded to the Ditchley estate in 1716 and, no doubt conscious of the status he was now called upon to maintain, pulled down the old house and commenced building the one that stands today.

The third Earl of Litchfield, a great-great-grandson of Charles I, married Diana Frankland, who was a great-granddaughter of Oliver Cromwell. Regrettably, there was no issue, for the result of such a union must surely have been exceptional.

Ditchley then passed to an uncle, who had thirteen sons but as none of them left an heir the estate passed to the third Earl's sister, Charlotte, whose husband was the eleventh Viscount Dillon. The Dillons joined 'Lee' to their name and lived at Ditchley, but the twelfth Viscount moved to Ireland rather than face his creditors, and about this period the house was let.

Subsequent members of the family, however, lived in the house. The seventeenth Viscount, Harold, died in 1932 at the age of eighty-eight, and was well known in the district as a fine man. Over a much wider area he was acknowledged as one of the most famous antiquaries in the British

A copy of Bernini's 'Apollo and Daphne'

Isles. An expert on armour and church brasses, he was for a time curator of the Tower of London armoury and a trustee of the National Gallery and the British Museum.

Most of the estate was agricultural and when the slump of the 1930s set in, finances were strained. Difficulties over death duties arose on the death of the seventeenth Viscount, most of the contents of the house had to be sold, and the 350 years of ownership by the Lee and later Dillon families came to an end.

In 1933 Ditchley was purchased by Mr Ronald Tree, MP, who restored it on a generous scale but in keeping with its architectural style. Sir Winston Churchill used it frequently as a weekend retreat during the early years of the second world war, and history was made when the details of Lend Lease were worked out there with Harry Hopkins, special representative of Franklin D. Roosevelt, the American President.

Having a few idle hours on a visit in 1941, Churchill was watching a Marx Brothers film when the news came of the arrival in Scotland of Rudolph Hess on a peace mission. Churchill sent for the Duke of Hamilton to report to him at Ditchley and when he had digested the details, commented: 'The maggot is in the apple.'

The architect of the house was James Gibbs, who had been responsible for many great public buildings, including the church of St Martin's-in-the-Field and the Radcliffe Camera at Oxford. He was assisted by William Kent, Henry Flitcroft and a team of Italian plasterers, but the mansion avoids the flamboyancy of its near neighbour, Blenheim, and its appeal lies in its simple, dignified Palladian-style proportions. Although the house was built early in the reign of George I, the date 1772 can still be seen on the rainwater pipes, and parts of the interior, including the fireplaces by Cheere, were not completed until some years later.

The full width of the house spans 350ft. Formerly the brewhouse, dairy and laundry were in the east wing, while the west wing accommodated the servants and included the stables. A rather startling touch to the facade of the house are the two life-size figures representing Loyalty and Fame.

The building accounts, which have been meticulously preserved, show that the house cost £9,000 to build, a figure less than the builder's original estimate. It is of interest that some of the materials used in the building were transported from Birmingham to Stratford by water.

Almost exactly a cube, the entrance hall is mostly the work of William Kent, including the large oval painting on the ceiling, portraying an assembly of gods and goddesses with Jupiter as the central figure. There are a number of figures on pediments and above these on brackets are some literary worthies. The gold paint for the gilding in the hall cost £13, and the mantlepieces averaged £100 each. Above the mantlepiece in the hall there is a portrait by William Aikman of the second Earl of Litchfield.

Four lions with foliated tails at each corner of the ceiling picture, and two eagles one on either side of a plaque of Alexander Pope, are thought to be Henry Flitcroft's contribution to the great hall. He charged £16 for the work, as shown by an account in his own handwriting for 'two birds and four beasts in the great hall'.

Opening off the hall is the Chinese or tapestry room, though today it contains neither tapestries nor anything Chinese. A fine picture of Sir Henry Lee, Ranger of Woodstock, by Marc Gheeraerds hangs here. He is pictured with his dog, Bevis, and a story goes that once when most unusually the dog refused an order to leave his master's bedroom, a search disclosed an intruder hiding under the bed.

Adjoining is the Genoese velvet room which was formerly a state bedroom. It owes its name to the magnificent Genoese cut-velvet wall hangings and curtains purchased in 1738 and still in splendid condition.

The white drawing-room is notable for fine portraits of Charles II and Barbara Villiers, Duchess of Cleveland, by Lely, which hang at either end of the room.

Ditchley does not boast the main staircase common to most mansions of this size, but the house is served by two—one at each end of the house. Both go to the first floor, only one continues to the second floor, certainly an unusual arrangement. Four smaller staircases are service ones and start from the basement.

On the first floor is the room known as the Queen's room, as it was used by the present queen on her visit in 1959, when she planted a tree to mark the occasion of her first official visit to Oxfordshire. Another room is decorated with William Morris hand-blocked paper.

When the contents of the house were sold in the 1930s most of the pictures went, too, though a few fine ones remain by Kneller, Wooton, Pannini, Highmoor and Russell, as well as the pictures already mentioned. Two fine portraits by Sir Thomas Lawrence have been loaned from the estate of the Marquess of Londonderry, whilst most of the remainder are on loan from the Phillimore collection and include works by Lely, Kneller, Pannini, Beechey, Vanderbank and Raeburn.

In 1947, the estate was sold to the Earl of Wilton and it later became the property of Mr David Wills who, not needing the house for his own occupation as he already had a residence in the neighbourhood, gave it to the Ditchley Foundation which he set up and in which he has always been deeply interested. With the gift went a handsome endowment to be used for long-term educational projects and the study of matters of common in-terest to the British and American peoples. The first conferences to this end were held at Ditchley in 1962, since when Foundation conferences have been organised from time to time to study some major aspect of public affairs within the scope of the Foundation's purpose. Usually the composition is equally British and American, with representatives of any other country in the world relevant to the subjects being discussed. Every effort is made to run the establishment as a private house, and to avoid any impression of a college or conference atmosphere.

It is fitting that this lovely house should be contributing to Anglo-American friendship for the Lee family were equally famous in the United States and a Lee property in Virginia was named Ditchley after a family home in England. The family who emigrated in the reign of Charles I later produced Robert E. Lee, famous general of the Confederate Army in the American Civil War.

A view of the gardens from the white drawing-room

DODINGTON

GLOUCESTERSHIRE

Historic home built by Wyatt

The great mansion, the Civil War which divided the family, West Indian plantations and the slave trade, and family dissension which led to long and involved litigation—these are but a few chapters in the eventful story of the Codringtons, whose lives for 800 years have been centred on this lovely corner of the south-west Cotswolds.

From the mid-fifteenth century the Codringtons were an important family. One member accompanied Henry V to the French wars and served at Agincourt, where he was standard-bearer to the king. A later descendant played a part in founding the colony of Virginia, another served in the Dutch war. It was, however, the English Civil War which caused the beginning of a rift in the family. Most of them sympathised with the king and when war became imminent John Codrington was called upon to raise troops for Parliament. He refused and instead took up arms for Charles I. After the battle of Naseby he was taken prisoner and his estates were sequestered. His brother, Robert, supported Parliament and at the Restoration, Christopher, a third brother, feeling that things might be difficult for him, settled his affairs and sailed for the West Indies. Under extremely adverse conditions, he developed virgin land in Barbados and eventually amassed immense wealth.

The family originally lived at Codrington Court, an Elizabethan mansion a few miles from Dodington. In 1796, Sir Christopher Bethell Codrington began to build the present mansion on the site of a Tudor house in which the family had lived since 1597. He employed James Wyatt for the purpose and it was all of twenty years before the building was finished, mainly because it cost £120,000 and was built out of income.

A great portico supported by six massive Corinthian columns fills two-thirds of the facade of the west front and dominates the rest of the frontage.

A conservatory curving away to the north and, beyond it, the church, combine to make an impressive group.

Originally the buildings surrounded a great courtyard, on one side of which were the servants' quarters, kitchens, an art gallery and a billiards hall. Below were the cellars in which was stored the beer made on the premises and said to be the best in the country. So huge were these cellars that a dray could be driven into them without difficulty. In those days sixty servants were employed, and account books which have been preserved show the wages of the coachman as £24 a year, and of the gamekeeper £5 10s. This portion of the buildings deteriorated badly with disuse and was demolished about 1930.

The portico leads to the entrance hall, which is 66ft wide and with the two halls on either side forms a double cube. The ceiling is made up of fifteen sculptured panels, separated by ribbons of oak leaves, a pattern cleverly repeated in red and white stone with black marble in the floor. Columns divide the side halls from the main hall. Above the fireplace is a fine portrait by Sir Archer Shee of Christopher Codrington. To the left of the hall is a door giving on to the stairs which lead to the church. These stairs are the only remaining part of the Tudor house which stood on the site.

At the rear of the hall a door leads into the superb staircase hall and, rising from the centre, is a double staircase, undoubtedly one of the finest in the country. It branches from a half-landing into two parallel flights and is joined at the top by a gallery. Graceful cantilevered stairs rise to the gallery, giving the impression that the whole is actually floating. The ironwork of the stairs was originally gilded and came from the great Fonthill mansion in Wiltshire. The iron balusters were specially designed to support the metal panels and to serve as standards for the original gas lighting which was piped throughout the house. The hall is lit by a roof lantern which rises to the height of the house, and the whole area is coloured in white and powder blue.

All the principal rooms are notable for the richness of their decoration, the marble fireplaces, doorheads and ceilings combining to enhance the effect. Piped gas must have been quite an innovation in 1796 but the house also had underfloor heating from ducts in the floor which were fed by hot air from the boiler house in the cellars. The massive mahogany doors, some 10ft high, are supported top and bottom, but have no hinges. Yet they ride as smoothly today as when they were built. This is particularly noticeable in a massive section of library shelving which serves as a door to the entrance hall.

The library, drawing-room and garden vestibule form a suite of three rooms. All are handsomely furnished and decorated, mostly with a Roman motif. The dining-room furniture was designed by Wyatt.

On the upper landing one of the bedrooms is exceptional in being octagonal in shape. What appear to be cupboards with three doors have been built across each corner but in the cupboards nearest the windows, the centre panels are actually doors which give access to short passages leading to other rooms.

Most of the pictures in the house are of members of the extensive family who have lived at Dodington. Much of the fine collection containing many original works of art was sold off at the end of the nineteenth century, when the then owner, through free spending, found himself in financial difficulties.

One family picture shows Lady Georgiana

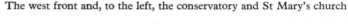
The west front and, to the left, the conservatory and St Mary's church

The staircase hall, showing the upper and lower galleries

Somerset, daughter of the seventh Duke of Beaufort, who married into the Codrington family. She was a great personality and hostess, who entertained Pitt, Wellington, Nelson and their contemporaries.

The story of the great house ended in tragedy for its creator. In 1813, Wyatt had been inspecting building progress with Sir Christopher, and they were speeding back to London when their coach collided with a post-chaise and overturned. Wyatt, struck on the head, was killed instantly, the owner escaping unhurt. Wyatt, therefore, did not live to see the completion of his work, though with the aid of his detailed plans, still to be seen in the museum, it was finally completed as he had envisaged it.

Of great interest are the records of payments signed by Wyatt in 1804, when the house was being erected. His own fees and expenses as architect amounted to £4,000. Other payments were:

Masons	£5,192	6s	7½d
Carpenters	£11,000	9s	6¼d
Plasterers	£2,694	8s	7¾d
Coppersmith	£611	19s	0 d
Locksmith	£328	9s	5¼d
Slaters	£1,209	12s	1¾d
Carver	£77	4s	0 d

The total of this particular sheet is £26,136 11s 8¼d.

When Christopher Codrington set off for the West Indies to make his fortune, he succeeded beyond his fondest dreams. Eventually, his son owned the entire island of Barbuda and much of

The entrance hall

his story is told in the fascinating exhibits on display in the museum, which is housed in part of the old cellars. Here one glimpses something of the vast gulf that existed between plantation owners and their unfortunate slaves, and there can be few more complete collections of material recording this dark period in British history than is shown in this museum. An extract from a book written in Codrington's own hand in 1715 includes instruction to one of his plantation managers to wait upon a ship's captain for:

'25 men, 5 women, 10 boys and 10 girls which I desire you will make a choice out of the whole number on board and mark them on the right breast with WC (his initials). Judy has the marking iron.'

This Codrington died in 1738, and in his will he made provision for what were, presumably, his offspring by some of the female slaves:

'To pay to his negro women, Judy, Flora and Rebecca Gee £10 apiece to whom he gave their freedom and to his mulatto boy Sam Gee, son of Rebecca Gee, £500 for two years after his death out of profits of an estate. The same applied to a mulatto boy Thomas, son of Sarah.'

The incongruity of the whole system is highlighted by the rule book of the Friendly Society which the owner set up to benefit the island. Subscribers paid 6d per month and in sickness they received 1s a week. As the society was intended to be a handmaid to the Church:

'the members do pledge themselves to give no countenance whatsoever to sabbath breaking, swearing, quarrelling, abusive or filthy language, lying, drunkenness, theft, witchcraft or dishonest dealing.'

In the case of persons extremely destitute from old age or some disease, and having no friends capable of helping them:

'it is recommended that such as these receive relief at a certain rate weekly all the year round.'

The Codrington family saw much service in the Indies. Christopher (1668-1710) followed his father as captain-general of the Leeward Islands. He was an unpopular governor and an appeal was made against him by the inhabitants of Antigua, whereupon he retired to his Barbados estates. When he died, he left £10,000 and books valued at £6,000 to All Souls College, Oxford. He also founded the Codrington College in Barbados, which became a renowned centre of learning and is still in existence. Part of the island of Barbuda he left to the Society for the Propagation of the Gospel in Foreign Parts.

Many members of the Codrington family have served with distinction in the Army and Navy, as for instance Admiral Sir Edward who, as a young captain commanded HMS *Orion* at Trafalgar in 1805, and in 1814, flew his flag on HMS *Chesapeake* at the taking of Washington. One son, General Sir William John Codrington, commanded the Light Division during the Crimean War and became commander-in-chief of the British Army, and later governor of Gibraltar.

In 1817, there was family dissension over the title and considerable litigation followed. A new patent of baronetcy was finally granted to Sir Gerald Codrington, son of Lady Georgiana Somerset and grandfather of the present owner.

Dodington, today, has become one of the foremost historical show houses in the country, with public attendance rising from 20,000 in 1969 to 200,000 within a few years.

A recently introduced feature is the carriage museum which is housed in the fine stable block built by Wyatt. There are over thirty vehicles,

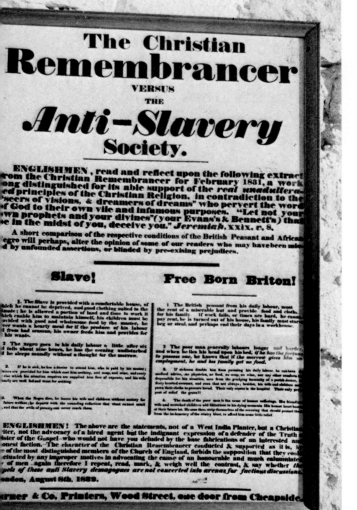

One of the many interesting documents in the museum. Dated 1832, it infers that the lot of the slaves was paradise compared to that of a British peasant

A fascinating museum is housed in the old cellars

ranging from dog-carts to resplendent coaches which once added a touch of colour to the main roads, as well as a landau, cape cart, governess cart, dray, brougham and a phaeton. The family travelling chariot, also on view, was used for a honeymoon trip early in the nineteenth century, during which it had to be transported, at some hazard, by raft across some of the principal rivers of Europe.

The present owner of Dodington is Major Simon Codrington, who resides there with his wife and three sons.

The acreage of the estate has not been reduced drastically and today comprises some 750 acres. There is a magic about the great houses in this part of the Cotswolds which seems to protect and keep them imune from the ever-increasing traffic which flows all around them, yet is neither seen nor heard. The M4 runs across one corner of the estate but, it might be fifty miles away for all the impact it has on this lovely mansion.

EBRINGTON MANOR

GLOUCESTERSHIRE

Home of a great chancellor

The old south wing

One of the loveliest yet least known villages of the Cotswolds is Ebrington, which lies some two miles east of Chipping Campden. The deeply-cut roads and lanes are flanked by an attractive assortment of cottages with thatched or stone roofs. Colourful gardens walled with Cotswold stone are set off by yews and other trees. It was here in 1456, close to the venerable church, that a Lord Chancellor of England bought for himself a house which his descendants have occupied ever since.

The first of this ancient and celebrated family to come to England arrived with William the Conqueror. He was Sir Richard le Fort and at the battle of Hastings he was quick enough to ward off with his shield an arrow which would have struck William. Whereupon the Conqueror commended him with the words *Forte ecu* (strong shield), which seemingly gave the Fortescues not only a name but a family motto, *Forte Scutum Salus Ducum* (a strong shield is the safety of leaders).

Records show that Radulphus Fortescue held lands at Modbury in south Devon early in the twelfth century. Two Fortescues took part in the Crusades with Richard I and yet another, Sir John, fought at Agincourt with Henry V. At that battle a Fortescue of the Norman branch of the family was killed fighting with the French men-at-arms. When Henry V died after the capture of Meaux, Sir John and his brothers-in-arms escorted the body of the king through France to England for its interment in Westminster Abbey, Sir John later returning to Normandy to become Governor of Meaux.

History, however, pays most attention to the second of the Agincourt warrior's three sons, John. Born about 1394, John's early years were spent in Devon and in due course he was sent to Exeter College, Oxford. His education completed, John quickly made his mark as an outstanding lawyer and served as a governor of Lincoln's Inn on three occasions. In 1442 he was appointed Lord Chief Justice of the realm and held office for eighteen years amid a rising tide of turbulence and riot, long enough indeed to be called upon to try the partisans of the House of York. We learn from the Paston letters that, three or four years before the disturbance reached its height, he sood in nightly expectation of an assault upon his house; but nothing came of it, 'the more pity' as the Yorkist

The main entrance as it is today

writer malignantly adds. At last, in 1461, the dethronement of Henry drove Fortescue from the Bench to follow the fortunes of his unlucky master abroad and on the battlefield. So abrupt a change of life must have been a severe trial for a man hard on seventy years of age; and as destiny ordained it, his first action was the fiercest ever fought by Englishmen, the battle between North and South at Towton. Devon man though he was, the old Chief Justice stood with his king on the

The Cromwellian balustrade of the gallery

Lancastrian side, fought through the long agony of that terrible day, heard the long shafts whistling through the driving sleet, and saw the battle sway in doubt for seven weary hours on the reddened snow. Then, at last, the Duke of Norfolk's column, like Blücher's at Waterloo, came upon the king's flank and after yet three more bitter hours swept his army in confusion from the field.

After the battle John Fortescue fled with the king to Newcastle and fought again in the several other hopeless actions which led up to the overwhelming defeat of the Lancastrian forces at Hexham. When, later, the king was captured and imprisoned in the Tower of London, Fortescue, already outlawed, escaped and followed Queen Margaret and her young son to exile in Flanders where he became tutor to the prince.

He returned with the royal party to England when Henry VI was temporarily restored to the throne in 1470 and was again with the king's forces when, in the following year, they met with their devastating and final defeat at Tewkesbury. The young prince, fighting violently, was slain on the field but Fortescue, taken prisoner, was later released, possibly out of respect for his age or in the hope that his talents might yet be of use to his captors. He was pardoned by Edward IV and restored to his seat on the Privy Council. His forfeited property, however, was not returned until he had agreed to write a pamphlet refuting an earlier one in which he had questioned the Yorkist title to the Crown.

Sir John then retired to the Gloucestershire manor and estate which he had purchased many years earlier. All his contemporaries pay tribute to his brilliance as a lawyer and all men have honoured him for his unswerving loyalty and faithful service to his king. In his lifetime there were eight kings of England and the transition from the Plantagenet to the Tudor line of monarchs. Yet he is perhaps best remembered for his legal writings, one of which, *'De Laudibus',* is still studied by legal students both in Britain and the United States.

He must have been a man of indomitable courage and physical toughness to have survived the vicissitudes of those turbulent times and, moreover, to live on to the then extraordinary age of ninety. He was buried in the church across the courtyard from his house and his tomb may still be seen.

Martin, one of Chancellor's sons, married an heiress, Elizabeth Denzil, and so came by the estates of Castle Hill and Weare Giffard in North Devon. Hugh Fortescue, father of the first Earl, married a daughter of Lord Aylmer and lived at Ebrington. Their coat-of-arms in stone is still over the original main door on the west side of the house. Lord Aylmer was commander-in-chief of the Navy and was responsible for the building of Greenwich Hospital School for the sons of seamen.

In the nineteenth century another Sir John Fortescue, who was librarian at Windsor Castle, wrote a monumental and classic history of the British Army.

Hugh, the fourth Earl, who lived at Castle Hill until his death in 1931, was a greatly respected figure in the West Country. The eldest of his three sons, also called Hugh, became the fifth Earl, and as a regular soldier served with the Royal Scots Greys from 1907 to 1921. He saw service overseas in the 1914-18 war and was awarded the Military Cross. He commanded the Devon Yeomanry from 1925 to 1931 and also served in the second world war. His only son, also an officer in the Royal Scots Greys, was killed just before the battle of Alamein in 1942.

On the death of the fifth Earl in 1958, his brother Denzil succeeded to the title. He, too, was brought up in Devon and was an extremely popular officer in the Devon Yeomanry, which he commanded from 1935 to 1941. He fought in Gallipoli

Hugh, 4th Earl Fortescue

and France during the first world war and, like his brother, won the Military Cross. Lord and Lady Fortescue have three sons and a daughter and Ebrington Manor is still the family home.

It is difficult today to visualise the house as it must have been when the great Chancellor lived there, for little of the original building remains. A block at the south end of the house comprising cellars and first floor is virtually unaltered from the thirteenth and fourteenth centuries, and was part of the house the Chancellor purchased. The rooms still have their fine coved and ribbed ceilings.

Through the centuries much alteration has taken place and most of the house was rebuilt in Elizabethan days.

In about 1830 the Elizabethan wings were demolished, the back door on the north side of the house became the present front door, and the frontage faced west. In the 1890s and 1920s there were additions on the east side which are unfortunately completely out of character with the rest of the house, and mar the beauty and dignity of the older building on that side.

Inside nothing detracts from the charm of the Elizabethan rooms with their panels and beams. The hall is a most impressive room and the open gallery above has a Cromwellian balustrade and panelling of Charles II period. The well-proportioned sitting-room is notable for its oak beams and most attractive pine panelling dating from the William and Mary period.

Ebrington church is but a stone's throw from the manor house and its recessed south doorway, going back to Norman times, is magnificently embellished with three variations of dog-tooth ornamentation. The ancient door still has its original hinges and a now rare bar-fastening in the form of an oak beam some 6ft long which slides into the wall. The fifteenth-century font is complete with its original steps.

The fine tomb of Lord Chancellor Fortescue is in the chancel. Carved, and coloured with fan tracery and shields, the life-size figure is shown wearing the robes of the office to which he brought so much honour.

The west front

OWLPEN OLD MANOR

GLOUCESTERSHIRE

A picturesque Cotswold manor

Nestling in a secluded wooded valley of the south-east Cotswolds is one of the most picturesque of all Cotswold manor houses, Owlpen. Throughout the years it has been fortunate in preserving its splendid isolation, and even today the approach to it from Uley village is along a single-track lane. From the house, the lane continues up a hillside with a gradient of 1 in 4 until the top of the valley is reached and with it a main road.

There has been a house in this lovely spot since the twelfth century, and though the present building dates largely from the sixteenth century, some of the roof trusses indicate that part of the structure is at least 100 years older. In records, the name of the family living there is spelt in many ways, the first reference being to Bartholomew de Olepenne in 1179. Thereafter the spelling varied to Oldpen, Owlepenne, Oulpenne and even, Wolpen. This was common practice even much later, for there are at least fifty recorded ways of spelling Sir Walter Raleigh's name, several of which he himself used.

The Owlpen family lived at the house until the fifteenth century, when Margery, grand-daughter and heiress of John, the last of his line, married John Daunt of nearby Wotton-under-Edge, and the house remained in the Daunt family for the next 300 years. Either the son or grandson of John and Margery Daunt carried out considerable reconstruction about the middle of the sixteenth century, when the great hall and the chamber above it were built.

The house passed from father to son uneventfully until 1719, when Thomas returned from Ireland with the intention of carrying out considerable improvements. He refaced the east wing and altered the rooms behind, but his greatest work was to lay out the gardens on a series of five terraces, and to plant a number of yew trees. These

grew to such good effect that they practically engulfed the house, so in 1950, after flourishing for some 200 years, many were removed to let light and air into the building. Some excellent yews on the second terrace still form an enclosure known as the 'yew parlour'. Thomas also designed the stone gateway and concentric steps at the front of the property, as well as wooden gates and a fence which have since been faithfully reproduced.

As a family, the Daunts did nothing extraordinary but lived as minor gentry and landowners until the male line died out in 1803. The house suffered a considerable period of neglect after Mary, the last Daunt heiress, married Thomas Anthony Stoughton, who had estates in Ireland. This couple lived for a time at Owlpen but finding the manor too small and certainly not grand enough, they then built Owlpen House, a magnificent mansion at the top of the valley to the east, with extensive stables, a park and gardens. The manor was not totally abandoned, however, for a caretaker lived there and the gardens were kept up. It was a whim of the owners to take guests down from their great new house to picnic in the gardens of the manor house. The old manor had the last laugh though, for Owlpen House was pulled down in 1955, and the material used for other buildings. Owlpen Manor survives.

Today the visitor comes suddenly upon the house around a twist in the narrow lane which is the only approach. The attractive white-painted fence and concentric flight of stone steps lead to what was originally the main entrance, and standing on a limestone outcrop well back on the third of five terraces which rise towards the hillside is Owlpen Manor, the lawn and gateway being on the lowest terrace. The first impression is of a house which vaguely resembles a squat letter H and there are many visible signs of the alterations and additions which have been made through the centuries to create the present building from the original medieval manor. There are clear indications that the house was considerably enlarged in the sixteenth and early seventeenth centuries, and it is known that the west wing acquired its bow windows and diminutive battlements in 1616. The last major alterations were carried out in 1719.

The central portion of the house accommodates the great hall, which retains many features of the Tudor period, including a six-light mullioned window. The main entrance was then in this central portion of the house and undoubtedly gave on to a screens passage which ran the depth of the house to a corresponding door on the far side. The massive timbers of the ceiling stop short at a line where the passage would have been. There is a Tudor fireplace in the hall and, above it and to one side, a small double window which lights the newel stair behind. An armorial fresco on the north wall marks the Daunt-Owlepenne alliance, and includes the owls as well as the Cornish choughs of the Daunts.

The oak parlour, entered from the hall through an original doorway, has a Jacobean bay extension. There were originally two rooms, but they were combined into one unit in a 1925 restoration. The fine oak panelling bears some unusual markings which appear to have been washed on—possibly an early attempt at graining or perhaps the panels were at some time painted. The patterns are certainly curious, some having the appearance of skeletons, while others accentuate the grain of the wood.

The typical Cotswold stone fireplace has a number of initials of the Daunt family scratched into it: TD (Thomas), KD (Kingscote), Achilles (an unusual name which was much used in the family), and many others, most of whom were seventeenth-century Daunts. The flooring is superb and again unusual. It consists of chestnut planks varying both in length and width, many of which taper off, fol-

The south front, showing what was the original front entrance

lowing the line of the tree from which they were cut. From the oak parlour, a fine newel stair containing some of the original solid oak treads leads up to the first floor.

Immediately above the great hall on the first floor is the great chamber, behind which runs a passage giving access to both east and west wings. That this chamber was once larger is obvious from the position of the windows, but at some time it was reduced in size to form part of another room.

Exciting, and now quite rare, are the wall coverings—a series of painted cloths of the kind which were imported from the Low Countries in Tudor times and were in general use in houses of this type. As a cheap substitute for the tapestries which covered the walls of the grander houses, they must have been quite common, so it is curious that they

should today have become so rare. With the exception of some fragments in the Victoria & Albert Museum, there are not more than one or two sets remaining in houses. The cloth, apparently a canvas or perhaps coarse linen, is 42in wide, the backgrounds being painted mainly in dark browns and greens, with buildings and figures in red, blue and yellow. It is difficult to tell how much the brightness of the colours has suffered in the 300 years during which they have been hanging.

The theme of the paintings is believed to be the 'Life of Joseph', and certainly the artist gave full rein to his imagination. In one cartoon Joseph is depicted being rescued from the pit, in another Jacob is admiring the coat of many colours. The background scenes of castles, strange trees which may have been cypresses, and other designs sug-

73

A corner of the great hall. Note the original six-light Tudor window

gest that the artist was recording his impression of the Holy Land.

It was of these painted cloths that Shakespeare wrote, when in part 2 of *Henry IV*, act three, scene one, Falstaff says to Mistress Quickly:

> . . . and for thy walls a pretty slight drollery, or the story of the prodigal, or the German hunting in water-work, is worth a thousand of these bed-hangings and these fly-bitten tapestries.

Opening off the great hall on the east side is the white parlour which, since it was altered by Thomas Daunt in 1719, has remained untouched. It was then that the panelling and sash windows were installed, with the top portions of the windows fixed and only the lower sections movable. The outside walls mark the extent of the earlier buildings and are several feet thick. Entrance to the parlour from the hall is through a white-painted wooden archway, flanked by Ionic pilasters, and the room itself contains an attractive shell-headed alcove of unusual design and construction.

Accounts relating to the work involved in the panelling of this room survive and show that the carpenter, one Henry Fryer, was paid £2 6s 6d for the work and materials used, the latter including nails at 1s 6d, glue at 1s 10½d, 5d for pitch, and 11s for hinges to the shutter and two new locks.

The original kitchen of the east wing has been modernised, except for the huge fifteenth-century fireplace supported by an oak beam 15in thick and with a span of 15ft. Also retained are a set of medieval charcoal braziers, consisting of three circular basins set in a stone slab. Charcoal fires would have been lit in these and a forced draught came from the three holes or funnels set near the floor. This is a rare piece of medieval kitchen furniture and in an excellent state of preservation.

Rare painted cloth wall coverings, which are 300 years old

Close to the house is a fine medieval barn of six bays with a cruck roof. Built of Cotswold stone, its massive roof trusses have weathered 500 years. At some date the barn was converted to a cider mill and, still to be seen, are the remains of the huge stone wheel on which another wheel set vertically once revolved to crush the apples, the motive power being supplied by a horse or donkey. The gigantic press stands in one corner, its two uprights being whole trees some 20ft high and so roughly shaped that the bark is still clinging in places. The main block of the press on which the screw operated is solid oak, 2ft 6in thick by 5ft wide. The screw itself is no less than 12in in diameter and cutting the thread must have been an herculean task. All this equipment was in use well into the nineteenth century.

To the south-west of the barn is a corn mill with its accompanying pond, fed by the Ewelme stream. There has been a mill on this site for hundreds of years, though the present building probably dates from the late eighteenth century. Though the mill is no longer in working order, the wheel was in operation into the late 1940s and much of the original machinery remains.

The water supply for the manor came from a stream which flowed down from the high ground behind the house and ran under the building. Outside the original front door there is a trap door beneath which the stream can be seen flowing only a few inches below ground level, and for centuries this was the only supply to the house. It was certainly no disadvantage for the water, pure, crystal clear and cold, is still prized by the owners.

Legends die hard and one still current at Owlpen claims that Margaret of Anjou, queen to Henry VI, stayed the night at the manor on her way to Tewkesbury in 1471, before the final battle of the Wars of the Roses, and that her ghost now walks there. The old house certainly stood then, though

75

the room with which her ghostly visits have been associated was a later addition to the manor.

A collection of medieval deeds and charters, lent to the Gloucestershire records office by a previous owner, are now back at Owlpen. They consist of marriage settlements and land agreements, and it is interesting to read names which are perpetuated in the names of villages in the district, such as Kingscote, Berkeley, Stintescumbe (Stinchcombe) and Ywelege (Uley).

To the west of the house and on the same level stands a Cotswold-stone building known as the Court House. Built in Stuart times, the single room of the upper storey is believed to have been the meeting place of the Court Leet. The lower portion, a simple loggia, served as a summer house.

The church immediately behind the house is built on the site of a Norman chapel. A later building was demolished in 1830 and a still later building was adapted to its present form in the 1870s. The chancel is remarkable for its elaborate mosaic work, and memorial brasses of members of the Daunt family, rescued from the former church, now have their place on the walls.

In 1926 Owlpen, by then very nearly derelict, was bought by Norman Jewson, an architect and one of the leaders of the vogue to restore Cotswold buildings. He decided that Owlpen was well worth rescuing and his beautiful and sympathetic restoration has demonstrated this beyond all shadow of doubt.

Captain and Mrs Crohan purchased the property in 1927, and in 1963 it was acquired by its present owner, Mr Francis Pagan.

Owlpen from the west

SNOWSHILL MANOR

GLOUCESTERSHIRE

A house of treasures

The approach to the house
from the south

A fine portrait of Charles Wade, who created the Snowshill collection

One of the lovely and as yet unspoiled villages of the Cotswolds is Snowshill, which lies some two miles from Broadway and is almost 1,000ft above sea level. The little church standing in the centre dominates the village, and a triangular green is bounded on two sides by cottages of Cotswold stone. The whole scene can have altered very little over the centuries. The village road winds from the church towards Broadway. On the right are more picturesque cottages, and on the left the manor house, built about the middle of the sixteenth century. The ground plot of an earlier building is fairly obvious from the irregular formation of the buildings round the inner courtyard.

Snowshill is a typical Cotswold manor house in most respects. Built of the local stone, it epitomises the best traditions of the Cotswold craftsmen. Its gables, stone mullions, the fireplaces and panelling are all of the quality and style expected of such a house in this area. The eastern frontage, which faces the village street, has very few windows, and the main entrance is approached from the south through two forecourts each enclosed by a protecting stone wall.

The manor of Snowshill was originally held by the Abbey of Winchcombe in 821 AD and it is recorded in the Domesday Book. When the Abbey was sequestered at the Dissolution, the manor passed to the Crown and four years later Henry VIII consigned it to Katherine Parr, as part of her dowry. On Henry's death Katherine married Thomas Seymour, Lord Sudeley, and when he was executed in 1549, the property again reverted to the Crown. Edward VI later conferred it on John Dudley, Earl of Warwick, but his attempt to place Lady Jane Grey on the throne cost him his head. The Crown then alienated it to Francis Bulstrode and it passed through various hands until 1860, when it is recorded that the manor house,

together with 1,226 acres, was sold for £26,000. The house then suffered a fate similar to so many of its kind at that period. Leased as a farm, it gradually became derelict over the years until, in 1919, it was purchased by a remarkable character who could fairly be described as an eccentric genius.

Charles Paget Wade came of a family who had large interests in sugar and cotton on the island of St Kitts and in the West Indies. He studied as an architect under Mr E. F. Bishop of Ipswich, and in 1905 became fully qualified. For a period he was assistant to Sir Edwin Lutyens, who was then planning Hampstead Garden Suburb, but ar-

Set in the hillside, Snowshill was once the property of Katherine Parr

chitecture alone did not for long satisfy this man of many parts. Poet, artist, draughtsman, engineer, antiquarian, he was equally proficient in every role and when he bought Snowshill Manor he proceeded to devote all his talents and energy to its restoration.

His personal contribution was the garden and in place of the cattle byres and farmyard at the rear of the house, he designed and brought into being a very beautiful series of terraced gardens. The house finished, Charles Wade then turned his attention to what must have been his first and best love, collecting, a hobby he began when only eight years of age. He followed no hard and fast line, and would purchase anything which took his fancy and had a story associated with it. Agents reported to him from all over the country and items arrived continuously. If he purchased a clock which had parts missing, he would set to in his workshop and make the needed pieces with his own hands. Whether it was woodcarving, painting or making scale models, he was an expert.

Gradually the house, and there are twenty-two rooms, assumed the appearance of a museum, whereupon Wade moved into the former bakehouse in the courtyard. The bakehouse had three rooms. One he lived in and the fire in the hearth was never allowed to go out. Next to it was his workshop, equipped to a degree that most craftsmen only dream of, and by way of a small stone turret stair he went upstairs to sleep. There were no modern amenities in the house, no electricity, gas or telephone. Tallow candles of his own making supplied the light. A bachelor, he was also something of a recluse, yet to those who did know him he was charming and generous. An incurable romantic, he would often adopt a dress of black velvet coat and knee-breeches, red waistcoat with gilt buttons and shoes with silver buckles. His hair he always wore long.

His search for items to add to his by now vast collection went on, and many items he purchased for a pittance must now be very valuable. Typical was a Japanese shrine, still on show, which Wade found in a London warehouse and bought for £1. Two ship models now on loan to the Maritime Museum at Bucklers Hard (Hants) cost him £200 each and he painstakingly refitted them to the last piece of rigging.

Once a year he spring-cleaned the house and its vast collection, using a mixture of oil and vaseline for the steel items which, he asserted, kept them bright and shining for twelve months.

Queen Mary visited Snowshill and on one occasion, having inspected the collection, she turned to Mr Wade's mother and commented: 'A wonderful collection but by far the finest item is your son.'

The collection remains much as he left it, except that its layout and arrangement have been greatly improved in the last few years. The rooms carry odd names as, for instance, Meridian, Zenith, Top Royal, Admiral, Nadir, Mizzen, Salamander, Dragon—and everywhere there are curious and fascinating items. Of considerable interest is an antiphonal, a manuscript book measuring 2ft by 3ft, which came from a fourteenth-century abbey. The words are on one side, with the notation on the facing page, and its large size was dictated by the need for it to be read by a group of people in a dim light.

The music room is remarkable both for the number and the rarity of the instruments it contains. There are harps, lutes, citterns, lyres and a serpent, together with its successor an ophicleide, as well as bagpipes, oboes, trumpets, hautboys, horns and bassoons. Even a hurdy-gurdy is included. The instruments came from Russia, Italy, France, Ireland, Portugal and, nearer home, Cheltenham parish church.

The great garret houses a profusion of bicycles. There are thirteen bone-shakers and three penny-farthings, as well as five early 'way wizers', a wheeled machine with a recording device to measure distances. Cheek by jowl are children's prams and tricycles. Perhaps the finest items, however, are in the collection of twenty-two scale-model farm waggons, each in the distinctive style of famous English counties. Commissioned by Mr Wade at a cost of £28 10s each, they are to a scale of 1½in to the foot and he painted each one himself. Quite hideous, though enthralling to the younger generation, is the array of Japanese Samurai body armour. Mr Wade bought the collection from a warehouse which had been bombed and, characteristically, spent two years studying the subject so that he could replace or mend pieces that had been damaged. This collection has been dubbed the National Trust's chamber of horrors. Appropriately named, too, is the room containing children's toys, for it is indeed a 'Seventh Heaven'.

In all, the house is estimated to have at least 10,000 different items on display—an unique collection and a fascinating record of days gone by.

It would be strange if a house with such a long history did not have a legend associated with it, and Snowshill is no exception. Its legend concerns a happening which took place in 1604. On St Valentine's Eve of that year, Ann Parsons, a fifteen-year-old heiress who was betrothed to the son of her guardian, George Savage, was sleeping peacefully in her guardian's house when all the male members of the Palmer family, who then owned Snowshill, broke into the house and abducted her at dagger point. They carried her off to Snowshill, where their friend, the local vicar, was waiting. As the clock struck midnight Ann became—not unwillingly we are told—the bride of Anthony Palmer. The brief ceremony had hardly concluded before her guardian and his henchmen appeared on the scene and, after a long chase to Chipping

The gardens overlook the valley

Campden, rescued the girl. Some days later the Palmers again secured her. Eventually the case was taken to the Star Chamber, when the vicar and the Palmers were charged with abduction. They replied that Ann was only contracted to marry her guardian's son when her mother died and left her £3,000. Alas, there seems to be no record of how the affair ended, but Ann's room, furnished in contemporary style and uncluttered with museum pieces, is today more or less as it was in 1604. One likes to think she lived there 'happy ever after.'

In 1946, at the age of sixty-three, Charles Wade ceased to be a bachelor and because of the size of the collection he and his wife found it more convenient to live in a cottage on the estate, rather than in the manor house. In 1951 he gave Snowshill to the National Trust and in 1953, Mr & Mrs Wade decided to return to the island of St Kitts permanently. But his thoughts were never far away from Snowshill and, sadly, when they returned for a visit in 1956, Mr Wade was taken ill and died shortly afterwards in Evesham hospital. His grave, between those of his two sisters, is in the little churchyard opposite the manor house.

Snowshill village street—a Cotswold gem

STANWAY HOUSE

GLOUCESTERSHIRE

A harmony in Cotswold stone

One of the most architecturally attractive family homes in the Cotswolds, Stanway House, with its tithe barn and nearby church form a delightful picture, especially when approached from the north. Both the house and the barn are built entirely of Cotswold stone and tiles, which have mellowed over the centuries to the warm glow that no other material can reflect to the same degree.

Today the centre of an estate comprising almost 5,000 acres of farmland and woods, the manor of Stanway belonged originally to Tewkesbury Abbey and the abbot's lodging was probably the present east wing in which there is a Renaissance doorway, now internal.

Somewhere about 1530, probably by a lease granted by the abbot of Tewkesbury, it is recorded that Richard Tracy, second son of William Tracy of nearby Toddington, became the owner. When he died, his will stipulated that there should be no funeral pomp, or Masses said for his soul, and he made no bequests to the priests because he believed merit to lie in faith, not in works. The Tracys of Toddington were descended from William de Tracy, one of the knights who murdered Thomas à Becket in Canterbury Cathedral on Christmas Eve, 1170. Overcome with remorse, he later went on a pilgrimage to Sicily, where he was struck down and died from a horrible disease.

The fates of subsequent members of the Tracy family are a reminder of how tenuous the hold on life could be in those days, for Richard died in 1569; his son, Sir Paul, in 1626; and Paul's son, Sir Richard, in 1637. In turn, Richard's three sons, who died in 1658, 1666 and 1677, each inherited Stanway but none had sons to succeed him. Stanway accordingly went to Ferdinando, younger son of the third Lord Tracy of Toddington who, on his death in 1680, was succeeded by his infant son, John, who later married Anne, sister of Sir Robert Atkyns, the author of *The ancient and present state of Gloucestershire*.

Still, as if exacting vengeance for the Tracy crime of the twelfth century, the Grim Reaper pursued the family. John was succeeded in 1735 by his son Robert, who died childless in 1767 and he, in turn, by his brother Anthony, who died in 1769. John and Anne, though having seven sons and five daughters, had no Tracy grandson: so on Anthony's death his daughter Henrietta, who married Viscount Hereford and died childless in 1817, became lady of the manor. Susan, who succeeded on Henrietta's death, married Lord Elcho, the son of the seventh Earl of Wemyss. Lord Elcho died before his father, so that his son Francis, Earl of Wemyss and March, became the owner of Stanway on the death of his mother in 1835. Thus the owners of Stanway have been the Church up to about 1530, the Tracys until 1835, and since then the Earls of Wemyss and March.

Lord Elcho, heir to the eleventh Earl of Wemyss, married Lady Violet Catherine Manners, second daughter of the Duke of Rutland, and was killed in action at the battle of Katia in 1916, while serving with the Royal Gloucestershire Hussars. It is their elder son, the present Earl of Wemyss and March, Susan Tracy's great-great-great-great grandson, who has leased Stanway House to his mother and her second husband, Captain Guy Benson, who served in the West Kent Yeomanry at Gallipoli in the 1914-18 war and was later intelligence officer to the 2nd Cavalry Brigade.

The earliest parts of the house as we see it today are probably the buttressed north end of the west front and the presumed abbot's lodging at the end of the east wing. No date can be given with any certainty as to when the present house was added, but it is believed that either the second or third generation of Tracys started the work between the end of the sixteenth and the middle of the seventeenth century. The great western bay window with its sixty lights containing 792 panes of glass is magnificent and, much admired, too, is the very fine gatehouse, though it is certainly not the work of Inigo Jones, as is sometimes stated. The great architect died in 1652, whereas the gatehouse is of a later date. Also noteworthy is the pilgrim scallop shell which appears on the gatehouse and is repeated on lead rain-water pipes and in other places over the house. This badge commemorates the first Tracy's pilgrimage and has been in the Tracy coat-of-arms from the earliest days of heraldry.

The south front is, in effect, a refacing, probably carried out in about 1640, of several buildings on different levels so as to make a single harmonised unit. The floor levels rise considerably from the great hall up to the abbot's lodging, though from the outside the windows make the buildings appear to be on the level. Another wing existed on the east side of the house, but this was demolished in 1859 when buildings were added north of the main house to make an enclosed kitchen court, en-

The main gateway. Note the pilgrim scallop shells

The east front, with its superb
oriel window

Sport of kings in the sixteenth century, the oaken shovel board

tered through an archway. Most of these additions were, however, pulled down in 1949, though the former kitchen and the archway still form a link with the main building. The eighteenth-century offices have been converted into cottages.

All the reception rooms are both spacious and well-proportioned. The great hall was entered by a screens passage, later replaced with a colonnade of Doric pillars. Among the furnishings, a magnificent shovel board, or table, immediately takes the eye. This was a popular game among the gentry in the sixteenth century and was played by pushing brass discs up the table, the score being dependent on the distance they travelled. This table is a splendid specimen, being 22ft 10in long, 2ft 9in wide and 3in thick. It was obviously cut from one tree as there is not a single join to be found in the top.

Almost certainly the oak was grown on the estate and one wonders just how old it must be, since such a mammoth oak could not have been less than 300 years old when felled. The table is a particularly fine example of medieval craftsmanship, and the more remarkable when it is realised that such a monster would have had to be split by hand, with one man working in a sawpit and another above.

Shovelboard was a Tudor game and it is recorded in the Privy purse expenses of Henry VIII that a courtier 'won eight pounds from the King's Grace' while playing the game. It is thought that the game was played by scoring one point for a disc within the first line, two within the second line, and so on. A disc over the end scored nothing. Only a poor imitation, shove-halfpenny, now remains, but this table is complete with the original brass discs each weighing 4oz, which are so rare today that no one really knows just how old they are.

Another rare item of furniture is a Chippendale exercise chair, rather like the frame of a sedan chair, with a massive seat supported by powerful springs. When gentlemen of that day were unable to take their normal exercise on horseback, they pulled themselves up and down on the handrails of the chair to the alleged benefit of their livers. This lovely piece had been relegated to the stables, from which it was rescued some years ago.

The drawing-room contains two rare Chinese Chippendale day beds surmounted by pagoda-style canopies supported on mahogany posts and adorned with bells and carved wooden frills. Dating from about 1745, these luxurious settees are covered with yellow Chinese silk.

Among the many other beautiful things to be found in the house are tapestries, china, porcelain and family portraits, including a very fine and recently re-acquired picture of three members of the Charteris family, whose mother was Susan Tracy, Lady Elcho. Painted by Romney, it has the most exquisite colouring. Many of the pictures, tapestries and other items came to Stanway from Gosford, the Scottish seat of the Earls of Wemyss and March.

Just across the lawns from the house and in front of the ancient church, there stands the magnificent tithe barn which experts believe may possibly be of late thirteenth-century origin. Some 90ft long and 30ft wide, the building has been kept in excellent condition and, apart from one of the twenty-eight half sections of the cruck frames which was renewed some years ago, the timbers, almost certainly oak, have stood for nearly 600 years. The curved braces and the crossbeams are 12in square. The roof soars to its highest point some 35ft from the floor and it is astounding that these timbers have been able to support for centuries the

One of the Chinese Chippendale day-beds

A particularly fine example of the tapestries

weight of a roof whose Cotswold tiles must be several times heavier than the more usual roofing slates.

For at least ninety years now, concerts, theatrical performances and dances have been held in the barn, which has a maximum seating capacity of 300 and amazingly good acoustics. The *Beggar's Opera* and Handel's *Acis and Galatea* with choir and orchestra, are among the great successes which have been staged there.

A notorious character who ended his days at Stanway was Doctor Thomas Dover (1660-1742) whose great uncle, Capt Robert Dover (1575-1641) founded the Cotswold Games. Thomas qualified as a doctor at an early age and when he contracted smallpox he cured himself by having twenty-two ounces of blood taken from him, after which he was given an emetic. The rest of the treatment was simple:

> I had no fire allowed in my room, my windows were constantly open, my bedclothes were ordered to be laid no higher than my waist. I was made to take twelve bottles of small beer, acidulated with the spirit of vitriol every twenty-four hours.

He practised in Bristol, then in 1708, abandoning his previous life, he sailed round the world on a privateeering expedition. During the course of the voyage, in which two ships took part with Dover as second-in-command, the privateers sacked the city of Guayaquil and stored their

Members of the Charteris family, a
painting by Romney

plunder in the church, where they also slept. Here they contracted the plague, which had recently ravaged the town, and within forty-eight hours of sailing 180 men were struck down with the sickness. Dover took charge and, treating them with the same remedy that he had himself used, but adding diluted sulphuric acid, he saved the lives of all but eight of the men, an unprecedented achievement for those days. The ships returned to England loaded with plunder.

The outstanding episode of the voyage, however, was the rescue by Dover of the castaway, Alexander Selkirk, who had been alone on the island of Juan Fernandez for four years and four months. The account of his adventures, told to Daniel Defoe in the 'Llandoger Trow', a Bristol tavern, formed the basis of the classic story *Robinson Crusoe*.

Dover then settled down as a respectable doctor in London and towards the end of his days, presumably because of his friendship with a member of the Tracy family, he came to Stanway, where he later died and was buried in the vault below the church. His grave was lost when the vault was filled in during the nineteenth century.

Dover's main claim to medical fame lies with his work in treating veneral disease with mercury, and his name lives on in Dover's powders, a mild form of his treatment for the plague, which are still sold for influenza-type ailments.

A view of Stanway House, with the late thirteenth-century tithe barn in the foreground

STOWELL PARK and COMPTON CASSEY

GLOUCESTERSHIRE

A fortunate estate

The entrance gates, which are flanked by gazebos

A succession of wealthy families have been owners of Stowell Park Estate, near Northleach, so that it has been possible to maintain it in a state of perfection over several centuries.

The origin of the estate is somewhat obscure and it has been said that the property was anciently called Stonewell, after either a stone-built well or from a spring which had petrifying properties. Cer-

tainly the church which stands close to the house is of early Norman foundation.

Part of the present house, at least in outline, dates from the time of James I (1566-1603) but a still earlier one which stood on the same site was occupied by an elder branch of the Tame family. At a time when England's wealth rested on wool, it was fitting, yet unusual, that the house of one of

The east front. The building to the left is the ballroom, converted from the stables in 1913.

the greatest of all the wool merchants should be set in the very centre of the source of their wealth. James Tame, who lived in the fifteenth century, rebuilt Fairford church and lies buried in its north chapel. His good works were carried on by his son Edmund, who died in 1534. But the family were as numerous as were their estates and property. There were Tames at Cirencester, Fairford, Tetbury and Rendcomb, where Sir Edmund built the church, and one of them probably built the first of the houses which have occupied the site of the present Stowell Park.

In 1608 they sold the estate to a family called Atkinson, whose daughter married Thomas Wentworth, the statesman, who later possessed Stowell. He became the first Earl of Strafford. John Howe,

This doorway on the east frontage was formerly the main entrance

93

member of a family of great parliamentarians, bought Stowell from him. A Jacobite and a zealous, if indiscreet, politician in the late seventeenth century, Howe was a controversial figure, and when he died in 1731 his son, later the first Baron Chedworth, inherited his estates.

The Howes were not very interested in their Gloucestershire property and their visits were infrequent, but they retained it until the early nineteenth century. When the last of them died unmarried in 1804 the title became extinct, trustees broke up the estate, and Stowell and Chedworth were purchased by Sir William Scott, judge of the Admiralty Court and elder brother of the great lawyer, Lord Chancellor Eldon. In 1821 William was raised to the peerage and took as his title Lord Stowell. His only son died before him, so on his death his daughter, Lady Sidmouth, inherited and when she died the property went to the Lord Chancellor. There is no record that he enjoyed his inheritance to any great extent, but when he died he left a fortune of £230,000 and income from estates, presumably including those in Gloucestershire, amounting to some £12,000 per annum.

So the Earls of Eldon owned Stowell and it was the third Earl, John, who spent most of his life there and between 1886 and 1898 enlarged the mansion which he preferred to his fine house at Encombe, in Dorset.

The building of the James I period, which was not over large, appears to have been added to extensively on both the north and east sides, and support for this theory is afforded by the distinct differences in the stonework, particularly on the north side. One window in the old section is well out of true, pointing possibly to a gradual foundation subsidence over the years.

Today the central doorway on the south side gives on to a terrace which extends the length of the house. The central doorway, surmounted by the Atkinson coat-of-arms carved in stone, has a Renaissance entablature on short Ionic pilasters. There were two nineteenth-century Doric arches set at right angles to the house but only one at the end of the terrace now remains. Also on this terrace is a particularly fine seventeenth-century dovecote.

Steps lead down to a lower level which, prior to Lord Eldon's sweeping changes, was the main approach to the house. At that time the main drive came from a side road north of the house, up to the front and then swept around the house to the stables at the rear. The present entrance was erected in place of the previous one at the eastern end of the house and has a Renaissance porch with Gothic detail. This, together with the wing, is of nineteenth-century origin.

The stained glass windows of the entrance hall depict the armorial bearings of families which have been associated with the mansion: Tame, 1520; Wentworth, Earl of Strafford, 1640; and Howe, Lord Chedworth, 1722. In the inner hall a carved stone fireplace bears the arms of Howe of Stowell, the Earl of Eldon, to which those of Lord Vestey were added in 1923.

The stables came into the reconstruction scheme later and in 1913 they were converted into a handsome ballroom with a large gallery at one end. The splendid carving on the gallery was the work of Lord Eldon. A badminton court has since been added at the rear of the gallery. New stables were later built to the south of the house.

Lord Eldon was of a retiring disposition and guarded his privacy fiercely. His dislike of being watched or overlooked led him to add the castellated effect to the house in order to prevent the servants, who occupied the top floor of the house, looking down into the garden. He was also a keen archaeologist and to the excavations he caused to be made on the site of the Roman villa at Chedworth we owe the fascinating scene it presents today. First discovered in the middle of the nineteenth century, the remains of the villa were presented to the National Trust in 1924.

In 1923 Lord Eldon sold Stowell Park to the Hon Samuel Vestey, eldest son of the first Lord Vestey who, with his brother Sir Edmund, had founded the Union Cold Storage Co, built refrigeration works in South America and Australasia and formed the Blue Star Line of refrigerated ships. He succeeded his father in 1940 and died in 1954. His widow continued to live at Stowell Park until 1967.

His only son was killed serving as a captain in the Scots Guards in Italy in 1944 and the present Lord Vestey inherited the title from his grandfather in 1954.

Lord Vestey, now joint managing director of the Union Cold Storage Co, is the fourth generation to continue the business which was founded eighty years ago, so further demonstrating the truth of the family motto: *E Labore Stabilitas* (Out of Work comes Stability). He is also a polo enthusiast and has laid down a ground in the home park.

Stowell is surrounded by beautiful parkland, and the formal terraced gardens which fall away from the house on the eastern side afford superb views of Chedworth woods and the Coln valley. The house is approached through wrought-iron gates between two stone-built gazebos set diagonally on either side, with panelled stone gatepiers.

In all, the estate comprises some 5,000 acres and extends from Compton Abdale to Fossbridge in one direction and from Chedworth Wood to Northleach in the other. One wall which bounds the main road for a mile or so is probably one of the longest and finest examples of Cotswold stonewalling in the area, and is kept in impeccable condition.

COMPTON CASSEY

A mile or so across country from Stowell Park and approached through winding lanes is Compton Cassey, today the estate manager's house. It takes its name from Sir John Cassey, who was Chief Baron of the Exchequer to Henry IV. Sir John, who died in 1400, was buried in the little Saxon church of Deerhurst.

Records are sparse until the 1640s, when the place is referred to as Casey Compton and a Thomas Mustowe is known to have lived there. Wills in the Gloucester library show that Thomas was the son of the Withington miller, who died when the boy was only seven years old, leaving him an inheritance of £5. In his 'teens, he set up in business and when he died forty years later he left goods, chattels and cash to the value of over £1,000. His purse and apparel were listed as being

The Doom paintings in Stowell church, painted about 1150

95

worth £61, cattle and other livestock £285, and sheep and lambs £235.

This house is much older than Stowell Park and at least two of the Howe family, including Sir Richard Howe, resided there before moving up the valley. Today, Compton Cassey is but a fraction of its original size. Prints of the house in Atkyn's *History of Gloucestershire* show that in 1712 it was a large establishment, with a great avenue of limes, a stable block (still intact) and a bowling green surrounded by venerable yew trees, the site of which is now occupied by a Dutch barn. Left derelict for two score years, what now remains of this fine old house, with its huge oak beams, bread ovens—and above all, its atmosphere—has been restored by Lord Vestey to something of its former glory. Today a gracious farmhouse, Compton Cassey still retains the ambience of its greater days.

Recently, when alterations were being made, it was decided to install a fireplace in a ground-floor room. Apparently the ghost of Compton did not approve and several times the fireplace, which had been securely fixed against the wall, was found in the middle of the room. Eventually the twentieth century conceded defeat and the attempt to introduce such a modern contraption was abandoned.

THE CHURCH

Close to the house is the ancient church, dedicated to St Leonard and a rare example of the Norman cruciform type, formerly completed by a central tower. It is also remarkable for its wall paintings which are among the earliest mural representations of the 'Doom' recorded in England. Painted between 1150 and 1200 AD direct on to plastered walls with a brush, the figures show the sensitive and skilful work of an obvious master craftsman. The design is elaborate and extensive, depicting Christ seated in judgement among his angels, and experts state that the arrangement of the hair and character of the vestments show it to be of Norman origin.

SUDELEY CASTLE

GLOUCESTERSHIRE

A setting worthy of a queen

Sudeley Castle and, on the right, the impressive ruins of the fifteenth-century banqueting hall

A haven of peace set in the lovely Cotswold countryside just a mile from the ancient Saxon town of Winchcombe, it is easy to associate Sudeley Castle with the panoply of state of the queens who have lived there. It is more difficult to imagine the plot and counterplot, cannonade and violence of war which was also the lot of Sudeley in the seventeenth century.

The history of the manor of Sudeley goes back to Saxon days but little is known of the fortified building or early castle which once stood on the site. Ralph Boteler, who fought in the French wars for Henry V and Henry VI, certainly rebuilt the place with money extorted from high-born prisoners he had captured and held to ransom. He became Baron Sudeley in 1441, and only the Portmare tower on the west side and the magnificent ruins of the banqueting hall remain of his building. Certainly he made Sudeley a splendid place, so splendid that it was coveted by the king and became royal property in the reign of Edward VI, remaining so for nearly 100 years until it was given to Sir John Bridges by Queen Mary, when she created him Lord Chandos of Sudeley.

The most intriguing of the many royal and important personages who knew Sudeley was without doubt Katherine Parr, sixth and surviving wife of Henry VIII. She was a truly remarkable woman. First married at the age of thirteen, she married again when her husband died six years later. This time it was to the third Baron Latimer, an elderly and wealthy widower who had been twice married. Long before his death, Katherine was attracted to Thomas Seymour, later to become Lord High Admiral of England, but would seem to have kept her feelings within bounds. When Latimer died, the way at last seemed clear but she had reckoned without Henry VIII, who had met her when he had visited her husband. He had but recently sent his fifth wife to the block and it is curious that a man of his type should have looked with favour upon a woman who had buried two husbands.

Then thirty-one years of age, Katherine was quite elderly according to the standards of the time and could certainly lay no claim to beauty. Small of stature, she had a frank, cheerful disposition and was an intelligent and accomplished scholar, being proficient in Latin, Greek and other languages: moreover a clever needlewoman. Not at all the type of woman Henry usually chose for his favours.

When Henry first made known his honourable intentions, Katherine is said to have replied: 'It would be better to be your mistress than your wife, it would be safer so'—certainly a frank and accurate comment on the situation. They were married in 1543, and Katherine proved a remarkable queen. She had the courage of her convictions as regards the religious controversies of the day and her successful intercession with Henry for the re-instatement of the two princesses, Mary and Elizabeth, to their rightful positions, shows her to have been a woman of integrity. Within a few weeks of the king's death, Katherine married Thomas Seymour, though this was not made public for some months. The match did not have royal approval and the jewels given to Katherine by her husband were sequestered by Edward VI, more to the chagrin of Seymour, one suspects, than of the owner herself.

Thomas Seymour was a handsome and commanding man but undoubtedly a rogue and a libertine. The young king made a grant of Sudeley to him when he was created Lord High Admiral, and he hastened to make it worthy to receive his bride. Katherine Parr, accompanied by Lady Jane Grey and Princess Elizabeth, travelled down to the castle in great state and there she lived for a year. A daughter, Mary, was born in 1548, but Katherine herself died seven days later of puerperal fever. The future nine-day queen, Lady Jane Grey, was chief mourner when she was buried in the chapel adjoining the castle. Seymour did not even attend. He was up and away to London to further his conniving to get the young king, Edward, into his clutches. Even while Katherine lived, he had shocked his contemporaries by his familiarity with the young Elizabeth.

There has always been a mystery about the child Mary, who was dispossessed of her inheritance and sent to live with relatives. Agnes Strickland, the historian, states that the child grew to be a wife and mother. Other authorities say she died in infancy. Still to be seen in Sudeley Castle today is the small room which was the child's nursery.

Elizabeth, when queen, returned to the castle on several occasions, once for three days when revels were performed there in her honour.

When the Civil War broke out Sudeley was owned by the sixth Lord Chandos, and during its course the castle suffered severely. In 1643, it was surrendered to Parliamentary troops, but recaptured by Prince Rupert shortly afterwards, though not before the chapel had been desecrated and used as a stable. The castle was regarrisoned and after the Royalist defeat at Gloucester, Charles I made Sudeley his headquarters. It was bombarded again in 1644 and surrendered to Sir William Waller. Lord Chandos was fined £5,000 for his loyalty to King Charles, though one-fifth of the amount was remitted when the castle was reduced to a ruin by the Parliamentary troops in 1650.

A ruin it remained for nearly 200 years until two bachelor brothers, John and William Dent, purchased the place and began a restoration On their deaths a nephew inherited and it was his wife,

Henry VIII surrounded by miniatures of his wives

The young Elizabeth

'Paradise to Purgatory' in five panels painted by William Hogarth

Emma Brocklehurst, who enthusiastically set about restoring Sudeley to much of its former glory. For nearly fifty years the work of restoration proceeded, while Emma busily amassed a collection of historical items and Victoriana. This remarkable woman was also a generous local benefactor. She built the church school and almshouses at Winchcombe, and did much to assure a water supply for the town.

Of the early castle only the dungeon tower in the west corner remains. The banqueting hall, built in the fifteenth century, is but a picturesque ruin, though it gives a fair idea of the former magnificence of the castle. The Cromwellians, in carrying out an operation which they termed 'slighting' the castle, all but demolished it.

Over the years of their occupation the Dent family have been responsible for a considerable amount of excellent restoration work and there is much of interest in the rooms now open to the public. A showcase in the hall includes such macabre items as a tooth from Katherine Parr's coffin, a piece of the sere cloth and a book of prayers and meditations owned by the queen. Naturally, the indefatigable Emma Brocklehurst saw to it that there was a fine collection of Civil War items, and these include wearing apparel of Charles I and a royal despatch-box captured after the battle of Naseby. Many of the castle's historical treasures came from Horace Walpole's collection at Strawberry Hill, sold at auction in 1838-40.

Not the least of Sudeley's many treasures is a collection of very fine and interesting pictures. Those in the great hall include: Rubens' *Holy Family; Pope's Villa on the Thames,* an excellent Turner; *The infant Saviour embracing St John* by Van Dyck; and another Rubens *The miracle of St Francis of Paula.* Another famous picture is *The Lock* by Constable, which was purchased by Mr Dent-Brocklehurst's great-great-grandfather from the Royal Academy exhibition of 1824, for 150

Henry VIII and his family, a painting by Lucas de Heere

guineas complete with frame.

Elsewhere in the castle are Van Dyke's *Charles I* and the *Tudor Succession* a work which was given to Walsingham by Queen Elizabeth. Hans Ewart, who succeeded Holbein as the court painter of Henry VIII, was the artist. Other pictures in the collection include *Elizabeth* by Zuccaro; *Grace before Meat* by Jan Steen; a *Self Portrait* by Joshua Reynolds, and *Triumph of Pan* by Nicolas Poussin, a picture commissioned by Cardinal Richelieu. Outstanding, too, is Lucas de Heere's portrait of Henry VIII and his family. Inscribed round the picture is the artist's description of his sitters:

A face of muche nobilitye loe in a little roome.
Fowr states with thyr conditions heare shadowed in a showe
A father more than valyant.
A rare and vertuous son.
A zealous daughter in her kynd what els the world doth knowe
And last of all a vyrgin queen to Englands joy we see successyvely to hold the right and vertues of the three

An unusual attraction is a considerable collection of original letters from famous people, including politicians, soldiers, royalty and authors. One of especial interest is a note written in 1864 by

102

Abraham Lincoln, giving a Miss Sally Taylor permission to pass through the military lines with her baggage to go South.

Focal points on the first floor are Katherine Parr's rooms, both tiny even by today's standards and overlooking the main courtyard. There is an excellent display of miniatures of Henry VIII and his wives, with a picture, purported to be of Katherine's child, as a centrepiece.

The library which overlooks the courtyard contains a fine sixteenth-century fireplace and the carvings which surmount the doors were the work of Grinling Gibbons. Amongst the pictures here are the *Rape of Europa* by Claude Lorraine and *The Artist's Wife* by Andrea del Sarto. There is also a very fine Sheldon tapestry on one wall.

Over the main stairway is an unusual painting by William Hogarth, the *Bridge of Life*. In a series of five panels, Hogarth has depicted the progress from paradise to purgatory, and the figure astride the bridge in the centre is believed to be a self-portrait of the artist.

One corridor contains numerous samples of exquisite needlework, including a tiny satin christen-

Marie Antoinette's room

103

ing robe worn by Elizabeth I. Also on display is a collection of clay pipes which have been unearthed in the district—evidence that the men of Winchcombe, once a famous tobacco-growing area, enjoyed their own produce.

A new departure is the Royal Sudeley exhibition, comprising a series of eighteen rooms in the dungeon tower, each one telling by sound, visual aids and clever lighting effects the story of those who occupied Sudeley in days gone by. It is a most realistic exhibition, culminating with the swish of the headman's axe as Thomas Seymour at last pays the price for his life of intrigue.

Pictures of the appropriate period and other relevant items are placed at various points to give added interest to the story as it unfolds. In particular, there is a most striking life-size study of Queen Elizabeth I, the work of John Hutton, who was responsible for the glass work in Coventry Cathedral. This has been transferred on to glass by a special technique involving a dentist's drill.

The real beauty of Sudeley, however, lies in its gardens, seen at their best when the courtyard is a mass of roses set against the backcloth of the ruined banqueting hall. The topiary garden has yew hedges 15ft high and meeting overhead to

Yew hedges which conceal wide tunnels

The old tithe barn—now a picturesque ruin

form tunnels which are wide enough to walk through. The herbaceous borders are at their best in high summer, and an extensive lily-pond is a meeting-place for ducks, flamingoes and the numerous other birds in which the present owner takes a special interest. Peacocks and a wide variety of rare pheasants and other exotic species are to be seen in and around the grounds.

St Mary's chapel, standing in the grounds close to the house, was badly treated in the Civil War but was restored by the Dents in the nineteenth century. Here lies Katherine Parr whose coffin was discovered just two feet below the ground in the derelict chapel in 1782. When it was opened, the body it contained was found to be in a perfect state of preservation but numerous subsequent examinations caused the remains to become decomposed until only a skeleton remained. Eventually, in the nineteenth century, it was decently buried in the chapel in a tomb designed by Sir Gilbert Scott.

Sudeley today comprises an estate of some 2,000 acres and the present owners, Mr and Mrs Mark Dent-Brocklehurst, have been the guiding spirits in developing the castle as a place of interest. So well have they succeeded that visitors have increased threefold within a few years. Mrs Dent-Brocklehurst comes from Kentucky, and their marriage in the chapel was the first to be celebrated there for many years. They have one son and one daughter.

WILLIAMSTRIP PARK

GLOUCESTERSHIRE

A House that was a marriage gift

Coln St Aldwyns, one of the loveliest of the smaller Cotswold villages, is situated by the River Coln, roughly midway between Northleach and Fairford and some two miles from Bibury.

The fine old twelfth-century church where John Keble's father was vicar for over half-a-century stands close to the Elizabethan manor house with its attractive gables and fascinating chimneys. It was for long the home of the family of Hicks Beach, one of whose members was created first Viscount St Aldwyn (1906). Built of stone, with a Cotswold stone roof and mullioned windows, it was a farmhouse for a period until, in 1896, Sir Michael Hicks Beach altered and enlarged it to serve as a country residence. His coat-of-arms is over the front door. The house, still in excellent condition and now part of a girls' school, contains seventeenth-century panelling, eighteenth-century doorcases and fireplaces, and a fine staircase.

The story of the family who lived at the manor house is closely linked to another house, Williamstrip Park, named after the manor and parish which lies some half-a-mile away. This manor was mentioned in the Domesday Book and it is likely that the name came from 'a strip of William's land'. A house has certainly stood thereabouts surrounded by a great deer park for centuries and members of the Hicks Beach family have owned it for nearly 200 years.

It was in the sixteenth century that one, Robert Hicks, a mercer of Cheapside in the City of London, prospered. He was elected a freeman of the city, became wealthy and was able to give his three sons a good start in life, which at least two of them turned to good account.

Michael, the eldest, was scholarly and became private secretary to Elizabeth I's great minister, Lord Burghley. He served him so well that when the great man died, his service continued with

Burghley's son, Robert Cecil, later the first Earl of Salisbury. Michael Hicks was knighted in 1604 and from him descended the ninth Baronet, Sir Michael Edward Hicks Beach, created first Viscount St Aldwyn in 1906. James I bestowed a baronetcy on the son of Sir Michael Hicks in 1619, and thereafter it would seem that the family lived quiet country lives and took little part in public affairs for some 200 years.

Robert's younger son, Baptist, also prospered, assisted no doubt by his brother Michael's influence at Court, to whose members he supplied silks and mercery. He was knighted by James I and enjoyed the distinction of being one of the first citizens to keep a shop after receiving the accolade. Perhaps the most lucrative side of his business, and the one to which he owed his advancement, was the lending of money. He lent sums varying from £25,000 to £150,000 to James I, and similar amounts to his successor, Charles I, by whom he was elevated to the peerage as Baron Hicks of Ilmington and Viscount Campden of Gloucestershire.

In London, Sir Baptist had a splendid mansion and it is said that the land on which it stood was won at a game of cards. Nevertheless, he built a sumptuous mansion near the church at Chipping Campden at a cost of £30,000. A feature of the house was the great roof lantern which he caused to be lit at night for the benefit of travellers. Sir Baptist died in 1629, and during the Civil War, when Parliamentary troops advanced on Campden from Broadway, his widow set fire to the mansion rather than let it fall into their hands. Today all that remains is the imposing gateway next to the church and some derelict buildings in the grounds, enough to show the scale and grandeur of the house which once stood there.

Sir Baptist was a generous benefactor to many

causes and did much to beautify the great 'wool' church where he was eventually buried. His finest monuments, however, are the lovely almshouses and the open market hall in the main street of Chipping Camden, both gems of Cotswold architectural style.

At the end of the eighteenth century the two sons of Sir Howe Hicks of Beverstone Castle, William and Michael, paid a visit to Netheravon, a house and estate in Wiltshire. There was good reason, for the elder brother William had met a charming young heiress, Henrietta Maria Beach,

and was setting out to court her, perhaps taking his younger brother with him for moral support. It was a great mistake for, in the event, it was Michael, the younger brother, who found favour with the young lady and who eventually married her in 1779 adding her name of Beach to his own. He was then twenty-three years of age and the manor and estate of Williamstrip Park was the marriage gift of the bride's father to his daughter.

William never married and on his death the baronetcy devolved on Michael.

After an active participation in politics, during

One of the gracious rooms

The octagonal game larder and ice house

The south aspect

which he represented Cirencester in the House of Commons, Sir Michael died at the early age of forty-five, leaving his widow with two sons and six daughters. Lady Hicks Beach continued to live at Williamstrip until her death.

Sir Michael was succeeded by his grand-nephew, whose son, Michael Edward, was destined to become a great politician and statesman. His introduction to politics was to follow his father into parliament as member for East Gloucestershire in 1864 when he was twenty-seven years of age, and from then on he had an outstanding career. A contemporary of such political giants as Randolph Churchill, Gladstone, Disraeli, Campbell-Bannerman, Haldane, and Salisbury, he was Chief Secretary for Ireland 1874-78, a member of the Cabinet in 1876, and as Colonial Secretary from 1878 to 1880 was chiefly concerned with South African affairs. He supported General Gordon against the government and was Chancellor of the Exchequer from 1885 to 1886, a position he held again from 1895 to 1902. From 1888 to 1892 he was President of the Board of Trade. He was created a viscount in 1906, and an earldom was bestowed on him in 1915. When he lay dying in 1916, news arrived that his son, Viscount Quenington (MP for Tewkesbury), who was serving in Turkey with the Royal Gloucestershire Hussars, had been killed in action on a frontier where there had been no movement for months. His wife, Marjorie, Viscountess Quenington, had died in Cairo shortly before. The present Earl St Aldwyn, therefore, succeeded to

| Michael Hicks (son of 6th Bart) Henrietta, wife of Michael | Sir Howe Hicks (6th Bart) Sir Michael Beach (8th Bart), son of Michael and Henrietta | Sir William Hicks (7th Bart) Lady Hicks, wife of the 6th Baronet |

Sir Michael (9th Bart) and his sister, Caroline Julia

Lady Hicks Beach, wife of the 8th Baronet, with William, her second son

the title from his grandfather, and is the second Earl.

Williamstrip is a pleasant house surrounded by extensive and lovely parkland. Probably the third to be built on the site, it was erected about 1720 and considerably altered in 1790 to plans prepared by Sir John Soane for Michael Hicks Beach. At that time an extensive wing ran westward from the courtyard and stables, and contained kitchens, domestic offices and servants' quarters. Further alterations and additions were made to the house in 1865. After the second world war, the present earl had this wing demolished and it has left the house much more compact and easier to run under present-day conditions.

Williamstrip faces west over the valley of the Coln. There are three storeys, three central windows and segmental bows on either side. The portico, supported by four Ionic columns, is approached from the terrace by a flight of wide steps. There is a square entrance hall with the drawing-room to the right and facing south. To the left of the entrance is a smaller sitting-room and, opening from it, the 'justice' room. The dining-room is beyond the drawing-room and also faces south.

Among the family pictures are a charming set of the Hicks boys and the heiress, Henrietta Maria, to whose hand they both aspired. A large picture of the lady herself is in the hall.

Among the many family mementoes are miniature gold spoons which were given to Lady St Aldwyn's grandmother, Lady Mary Frances Dawson-Damer, a daughter of the fourth Earl of Portarlington. An accompanying picture shows her to have been a very beautiful woman. She was a great friend of a prince of the Russian royal family, whose presents to her included an Easter egg from the Fabergé workshops. She was a lady-in-waiting to Queen Alexandra and when she accompanied her to the opera she invariably received her own ovation after that to the queen.

In the courtyard there is an unusual game larder in an excellent state of preservation. It is octagonal in shape and the sills of the recessed arches, inserted into the building, were receptacles for ice which, as it melted, drained away through wire mesh. The conical roof was so designed that its open sides kept cool anything which was hoisted up in a special basket.

The estate, some 3,000 acres in extent, includes several farms, and the earl's prize-winning flock of 350 pedigree Suffolk sheep is the largest in the country.

The present Earl St Aldwyn, who was born at Sudeley Castle, served as a major in the Royal Gloucestershire Hussars. In 1958 he was appointed Chief Whip of the House of Lords. The position carries with it the post of captain of the Gentlemen at Arms, a body formerly known as the band of gentlemen pensioners, which was originally founded as a personal guard for Henry VIII. Lord and Lady St Aldwyn have three sons, the eldest of whom is Viscount Quenington.

Houses open to the public

The following are open to the public at certain times of the year:

Berkeley Castle, Gloucestershire

Blenheim Palace, Oxfordshire

Broughton Castle, Oxfordshire

Chastleton House, Gloucestershire

Compton Wynyates, Warwickshire

Dodington, Gloucestershire

Snowshill (National Trust), Gloucestershire

Sudeley Castle, Gloucestershire

Acknowledgements

The majority of the pictures were taken by the author, by kind permission of the owners of the properties. He wishes also to acknowledge with thanks the following sources of other illustrations:

The Marquess of Northampton: the exterior and drawing-room, Compton Wynyates, pages 49, 52

A. M. Illingworth, Esq: aerial view of Blenheim, page 26

Messrs Blinkhorn, Banbury: Broughton Castle floodlit, page 33

Major S. F. B. Codrington: staircase showing upper and lower galleries, Dodington, page 62

National Portrait Gallery, London: *Henry VIII and his Family* by Lucas de Heere, from the collection of the late Mark Dent-Brocklehurst, page 102

Biographical notes on artists and craftsmen mentioned in the text

ADAM, Robert (1728-92). Scottish architect. Studied in Edinburgh and Italy. Architect of the King's Works. Established London practice in 1758. Worked with his brother, James. Greatest project was building the Adelphi, London. Built as a speculation, it nearly ruined them and was finally disposed of by a lottery. The brothers also designed furniture and fittings to suit the houses they planned.

AIKMAN, William (1682-1731). Scottish portrait painter. Studied law and, later, painting under Sir John Medina. Visited Italy 1707. Returned to Scotland 1712 and met much encouragement as a portrait painter, the art form in which he excelled. Went to London 1723. An intimate of Kneller.

BALDUCCI, Matteo (-?-) Painter of altar pieces and religious subjects.

BATONI or BATTONI, Pompeo Giralamo (1708-87). Italian painter. First followed his father's profession of goldsmith. Studied painting in Rome, particularly Raphael's works. Painted historical works but chiefly portraits, including those of twenty-two monarchs. His pictures, and particularly heads, were very popular, and most European capitals have some of his works.

BEECHEY, Sir William (1753-1839). Portrait painter. Born: Oxfordshire. Knighted 1798. Two of his sons became admirals and two painters.

BROWN, Lancelot (1715-83). Born: Northumberland. Known as 'Capability' Brown. Landscape gardener and architect. Originally a kitchen gardener. Remarkable for his powers of prejudging landscape effects. Remodelled the grounds of Kew and Blenheim.

CASSELLI, Cristofore (Fifteenth-sixteenth centuries). Pupil of Mazznola. Earned livelihood as journeyman at Venice, where he painted an altar piece now in sacristy of Santa Maria della Salute. In 1496 became master at Palma. Dates of birth and death uncertain.

CHEERE, Sir Henry (1703-81). Sculptor. Pupil of Peter Scheemakers. Worked in marble, bronze and lead. Created baronet 1766.

CHIPPENDALE, Thomas (1718-79). English cabinet-maker. Born: Worcestershire. Set up business in St Martin's Lane, London, 1753, and quickly became famous for his graceful furniture, mostly made of mahogany, then a newly introduced wood. His designs influenced other craftsmen. Buried: St Martin's-in-the-Field.

CONSTABLE, John (1776-1837). English landscape painter. Born: Suffolk. Artistic triumph of his life was the public applause which greeted his *Haywain* in Paris 1821. A number of his work's are in the National Gallery and the Tate Gallery.

COTES, Francis (1725-70). English portrait painter. Born: London. Lord Orford compared some of his works in crayon to those of Rosalba.

D'AGNOLO, Andrea, Andrea Del Sarto (1487-1531). Italian painter. Born: Florence. Showed early aptitude for drawing and was placed with goldsmith to learn craft of engraving. Famous for beautiful landscape backgrounds. Among his finest works are frescoes illustrating the life of St John the Baptist. Honoured by Francis I of France in Paris, he painted many works, among them *Charity* which is now in the Louvre. In 1519 the king allowed him to return to Florence and gave him a commission to purchase works of art which he ignored, breaking every bond of honesty. Died of plague in Florence.

DE HEERE, Lucas (1534-84). Flemish painter of portraits and historical subjects. Born: Ghent. Employed at Fontainbleu by the Queen Mother, Catherine de Medici, in designing tapestries for the royal residences. In England, 1554, when he painted fine portrait of Queen Mary. Returned to Ghent and married wealthy young Protestant lady whose beauty and learning captivated him. Fled to Britain 1567 to escape religious persecution and there painted the remarkable allegorical portrait of Queen Elizabeth now at Hampton Court. Besides paintings in oil, he completed a collection of watercolours.

DE VOS, (mid-seventeenth century). Lived at Antwerp. Little recorded about him but his *Portrait of a Man* is in the Rotterdam Museum.

DE WINT, Peter (1784-1849). English water-colour painter. Born: Stone (Staffs). Intended to follow his father as a physician but studied under John Raphael Smith, the engraver. Entered schools of Royal Academy 1807. Rarely left England. Occasionally painted in oils and four of these, plus a large collection of water-colours, are in the South Kensington Museum. Died: London. Buried: Savoy Chapel.

FLITCROFT, Henry (1679-1769). English architect. Born: Hampton Court, where his father was king's gardener. Became Comptroller of Works in 1758. Designed several London churches and rebuilt part of Woburn Abbey.

GAINSBOROUGH, Thomas (1727-1788). Portrait and landscape painter. Born: Sudbury, Suffolk. One of England's great masters. Rival of Sir Joshua Reynolds. He settled as a portrait painter at Ipswich in 1745. Later moved to Bath where he won public acclaim with his portrait of Mr Nugent. One of his most famous pictures, *The Blue Boy*. He is represented in the National Gallery by fourteen works. He never signed and rarely dated his work. Buried: Kew.

GHEERAERDTS, Marc (1561-1635). Court painter to Elizabeth and James I.

GIBBONS, Grinling (1648-1720). Sculptor and woodcarver. Born: Rotterdam. Appointed by Charles II to a place on the Board of Works and was Master Carver until the time of George I. Responsible for carvings in the chapel of Windsor and the choir stalls at St Paul's. His work is also in many Wren churches in London. At many country mansions he executed a considerable amount of carved embellishment. A speciality of his woodcarvings lay in pendant groups and festoons of flowers, fruit, etc, carefully copied from nature. It is conceded he could not have executed all the work attributed to him by his own hands and he employed numerous carvers to carry out his designs. Married, he had nine children. Buried: St Paul's, Covent Garden.

GIBBS, James (1682-1754). British architect. An Aberdonian, he went to London in 1709. His great works included Radcliffe Library, Oxford, Senate House, Cambridge and St Martin's-in-the-Field.

GIORGIONE (c 1478--1511). Italian painter. His pictures were of great beauty and richness of colouring. He was the first exponent in Venice of the small picture in oils. When he died of the plague, many of his pictures are believed to have been completed by Titian.

HAWKSMOOR, Nicholas (1661-1736). Architect. Clerk to Sir Christopher Wren and also assisted Vanbrugh. Responsible for many London churches.

HIGHMORE, Joseph (1692-1780). Painter of portraits and historical subjects. First articled to an attorney. Later studied under Sir Godfrey Kneller (qv). Responsible for many royal portraits.

HOGARTH, William (1697-1764). Born: Smithfield, London. Apprenticed to a goldsmith but began engraving in 1720. In this he was successful but tiring, of conventional art, he turned to pictured morality. He had an acute eye for human foibles which he often recorded to the point of coarseness. Eloped with and married daughter of Sir James Thornhill (qv). His first great success was *Harlot's Progress* depicting the downfall of a country girl in London.

HOLBEIN, Hans, the younger (1497-1543). German painter. Studied under his father and became successful. Left Europe because of the religious trouble and came to London in 1526. Entered service of Henry VIII *circa* 1533. Died of the plague in London.

HOPPNER, John (1758-1810). Portrait painter. Born: Whitechapel of German parents. Was only rival to Sir Thomas Lawrence as a fashionable portrait painter. Between them they painted most of the fashionable society. Appointed Portrait Painter to the Prince of Wales, 1789. Buried: Hampstead, London.

HUDSON, Thomas (1701-1779). Portrait painter. Born: Devonshire, probably Bideford. A pupil to an artist, he made a runaway marriage with his master's daughter and adopted the profession of portrait painter. Joshua Reynolds was apprenticed to him. He became very successful and much in demand. His finest work is the family group of Charles, Duke of Marlborough, at Blenheim. Died at Twickenham.

KENT, William (1684-1748). Painter, sculptor, architect and landscape gardener. Built Horse Guards and Treasury buildings in London.

KNELLER, Sir Godfrey (1646-1723). Portrait painter. Born: Lubeck, Germany. Original name Gottfried Kniller. Destined for military life but love of painting drove him to Amsterdam. Came to London 1676 and four years later was Court Painter to Charles II. Subsequently he received royal favour from James II, William (who knighted him) and George I, who created him a baronet. In all, ten reigning sovereigns sat for him. The adulation he received made him extremely vain and arrogant, as well as extremely wealthy. Among his best known works are *Beauties of Hampton Court* painted for William III. Kept many assistants to whom were delegated the less important parts of his pictures. Died at Twickenham and buried in his own garden at Whitton, Twickenham. At his death, there were 500 unfinished portraits on hand.

LAGUERRE, Louis (1663-1721). French painter. Came to England 1684 and did work at Chatsworth. Blenheim is considered his best work.

LELY, Sir Peter (1618-1680). Portrait painter. Born: Westphalia, Originally named Pieter van de Faes. Came to London 1641 in train of William of Orange. Employed by Charles I and Cromwell, and Court Painter to Charles II, who knighted him in 1679. His paintings of Court beauties, including Nell Gwynne, are particularly famous. Buried: St Paul's, Covent Garden. His own collection of pictures, which included several old masters, was sold at his death for £26,000.

MARSHALL, Benjamin (1767-1835). English animal painter. He worked in London and Newmarket, his speciality being horses.

MORRIS, William (1834-96). Poet and artist. Born: Walthamstow, London. Close friend of Burne-Jones. He started painting but turned to poetry. In 1861, with friends, founded an establishment for the manufacture of wallpapers, stained glass, tiles and artistic decorations, which largely contributed to the reform of English taste in colour and design.

NASH, John (1752-1835). Architect. Born: London. Chiefly celebrated for his London street improvements. Regent Street and Brighton Pavilion were his work.

ORPEN, Sir William (1878-1931). British painter. Did much work at the front in 1914-18 war. Official painter at Paris peace conference. His portraits are accepted as among the finest work of his time.

PALMEZZANO, Marco (1456-?) Born Forlie. Pupil of Melozzo da Forli. He signed his early pictures 'Marcus de Melotius' which has resulted in many of his best paintings being attributed to his master. Responsible for several great altar pieces. *The Entombment* is in the National Gallery, London, but other works are to be found in the principal galleries of Europe.

PANNEMAKER. An outstanding Brussels family in the craft of weaving tapestries. Three of them were Franc (1679-84), Pet (1519-51), Willem (1539-69). A magnificent set of ten large tapestries woven by Willem Pannemaker, glorifying his patron the Holy

Roman Emperor, Charles V, is now in the Spanish State collection,

PANNINI. Giovanni Paolo (1692-1765). First painter to specialise in ruins, His paintings had an enormous vogue among tourists.

POUSSIN. Nicolas (1594-1665), Painter. Born: France. Painter to Louis XIII. Annoyed by court intrigues, he returned to Rome.

RAEBURN, Sir Henry (1756-1823). Portrait painter. Born: Edinburgh. First apprenticed to a goldsmith but began producing water-colour miniatures, then oils. Married a wealthy widow when twenty-two years of age. Attained pre-eminence among Scottish artists. For thirty years he enjoyed unbroken professional and social success and was knighted by George IV (1822). His style was akin to Reynolds. Most of his pictures are to be found in Scottish country houses. One of his most famous pictures. *The Macnab*, sold in 1917 for £25,400. Buried: Edinburgh.

REYNOLDS, Sir Joshua (1723-1792). Artist. Born: Plympton. The seventh son of a clergyman. At thirty-seven years of age he was at the height of his fame. Knighted in 1769 by George IV, he became Painter to the King in 1784. His portraits have never been surpassed. the finest being that of Mrs Siddons as *The Tragic Muse*. He was Mayor of Plymouth, 1733. He became partially blind and ceased to paint in 1789, by which time he had been responsible for between 2,000 and 3,000 works of art. He was the greatest portrait painter England has produced and one of the greatest of the world. Died in London. Buried: St Paul's.

ROMANO GUILIO—GIANNVZZI DEI (1492-1546). Apprenticed to Raphael and assisted him in the Vatican, where he was considered his best pupil. Raphael bequeathed his implements and works of art to him jointly with Gianfrancisco Penni. Accepted post of architect to St Peter's at Rome in succession to San Gallo and was about to set out for Rome when he died at Mantua.

RUBENS, Peter Paul (1577-1640). Artist. Born: Westphalia. Was intended for the Law but became a diplomat. Was despatched on a mission to Philip III of Spain and while at Madrid produced some portraits. His masterpiece, painted 1611-14, is generally accepted as the *Descent from the Cross*, now in Antwerp Cathedral. Was appointed envoy to Charles I to treat for peace in 1629, a delicate negotiation which he carried out with tact and success. His *Peace and War* is in the London National Gallery. He also made sketches for the banqueting hall at Whitehall. Knighted by Charles I and also by Philip IV of Spain. Main characteristics of his work—power, spirit and exuberant life.

ROMNEY, George (1734-1802). Portrait painter. Born: Dalton-in-Furness. First worked at his father's trade as a cabinetmaker. Was apprenticed at Kendal to be taught the art of a painter and in 1762 set up his easel in London, leaving behind his wife and two children. In the year 1786, he made 3,500 guineas by portrait painting. Lady Hamilton was painted in thirty differing characters. The highest price he ever received for a portrait was 120 guineas, yet in 1896 one of his works was sold for 10,500 guineas. In 1799 he was practically insane and returned to his wife at Kendal, where he died.

RUSSELL, John (1745-1806). English portrait painter. Born: Guildford (Surrey). Received tuition under Francis Cotes (qv). In London, he developed strong religious convictions and was responsible for portraits of the evangelists, George Whitfield and Charles Wesley. These were engraved and enjoyed a steady sale but the originals have never been discovered. He became King's Painter in 1789 and was considered the great portrait painter of the latter part of the eighteenth century. He worked almost always in pastels. His son, William, became a portrait painter of some note.

RYSBRACK, Michael (1693-1770). Sculptor. Born: Antwerp. Settled London 1720. Best works included Sir Isaac Newton's monument in Westminster Abbey and one to the Duke and Duchess of Marlborough at Blenheim.

SARGENT, John Singer (1856-1925). American portrait painter. Son of a physician. Trained in Florence and Paris. Settled in London 1884. He painted high society in Edwardian and Georgian periods. Had a prolific output of both lively portraits and brilliant water-colours.

SHEE, Sir Martin Archer (1769-1850). Portrait painter. Born: Dublin. Knighted 1830. In addition to painting he wrote poems, a novel and a play.

SMITH, Bernard (1630-1708). Known as Father Smith; born in Germany. Came to England 1660 as an organ builder, when efforts were being made to revive organ building in England. His first instrument was for Whitehall banqueting room. Became organ maker to Charles II and went on to immense success, being responsible for some fifty instruments mostly in churches.

SOANE, Sir John (1753-1837). English architect. Son of a mason. Went to Rome as travelling student. Contracted wealthy marriage. Architect of Bank of England. His art collection was presented to the nation. Founded Soane Musuem, London.

STUBBS, George (1724-1806). English painter who first studied and taught anatomy at York hospital. Specialised in animals. particularly horses. Also achieved distinction in sporting subjects. He experimented with enamel, fired on copperplates, or on Wedgwood china plaques.

THORNHILL, Sir James (1675-1734). Artist. Born: Melcombe Regis. Dorset. Responsible for painting the dome of St Paul's as well as much of the work at Blenheim, Hampton Court and Greenwich Hospital, on which he was employed for twenty years. Hogarth was one of his pupils. Unusually for an artist, he was Member of Parliament for Melcombe Regis, Dorset, for twelve years. Knighted by George I in 1720. A daughter married William Hogarth.

TURNER, Joseph Mallord William (1775-1851). English painter. Great master of landscape and of water-colour. Born: Covent Garden, London. Though almost illiterate, his genius was obvious and he entered the Royal Academy of Arts at fourteen. He was elected a Royal Academician at twenty-eight. Never married and led secretive private life. On his death, he bequeathed 300 paintings and 20,000 watercolours to the nation.

VANBRUGH, Sir John (1664-1726). Architect. Grandson of Protestant refugee from Ghent. Born: London. Educated in France, served with British regiment. Imprisoned in the Bastille. Successful playwright. Achieved success as an architect with Castle Howard (1702) and three years later commissioned to design Blenheim Palace.

VANDERBANK, Peter (1649-1697). Engraver. Born: Paris. Came to England in 1674 where he gained great reputation as engraver of portraits. His prints always bore the name spelt 'Vandrebanc'. Was buried at Bradfield, Hertfordshire.

VAN DYCK, Sir Anthony (1599-1641). Artist. Born: Antwerp. Son of a silk and woollen manufacturer. Began studying as a painter in his fifteenth year under Rubens. Made a brief visit to England in 1620. In 1632 returned to London and was received by Charles I, who knighted him and made him his Painter-in-Ordinary with a pension of £200. Altogether he painted twenty-eight portraits of the king. His greatest picture was *The Adoration of the Shepherds*. From 1636 he was in England for five years, during which time he painted nearly every distinguished person at Court.

VAN DE VELDE, Willem. There were two, father and son. The elder, born at Leyden in 1610, was a sailor in early life but soon acquired a reputation as a painter of marine subjects. The States of Holland put a vessel at his disposal to witness seafights. Invited to England, he received a pension from Charles II which was continued by James II. He died 1693 and was buried at St James, Piccadilly.

William (the younger) was born at Amsterdam in 1633, and early achieved success as an artist. He accompanied his father to London 1674. He, too, had a pension from Charles II and his successor. A prolific painter who worked at lightning speed, over 300 of his works were catalogued. The great majority are in English private collections, and some fourteen are in the National Gallery. Many of the seafights signed by the father were painted by the son from the father's designs. The twelve large naval engagements at Hampton Court, dated 1676 and 1682, are believed to be the work of the younger man.

VERMUYDEN, Sir Cornelius. The Dutch engineer who drained the Bedford Level in the mid-seventeenth century.

VERRIO, Antonio (1639-1707). Painter. Born: Italy. Charles II sent for him to re-establish the Mortlake tapestry works. Painted the ceilings of Windsor Castle. He was employed at Chatsworth and other country mansions. Enjoyed the favour of James II, William III and Queen Anne. Towards the end of his life his sight failed him. He died at Hampton Court.

WISE, Henry (1653-1738). Gardener to William III, Anne and George I, and responsible for the gardens of many great houses. In 1709, he purchased estate and mansion of the Priory, Warwick, where he lived until his death. Left £200,000.

WISSING, Willem (1656-87). Portrait painter. Born: Amsterdam. Came to England 1680 and was for a time assistant to Sir Peter Lely (qv), after whose death he became favourite of English patrons. Was a favourite painter of James II and painted all the royal family. Had reputation for flattering his lady sitters. Died while painting a portrait of Earl of Exeter.

WOOTTON, John (1678?-1765). Eminent English landscape and animal painter. Excelled in sporting pictures, dogs and horses. Was much employed at Newmarket, painting racehorses. In his latter years his sight failed. Died in London. Numerous examples of his work are in English country houses. Several are in the Royal collection and there are some admirable hunting scenes at Longleat.

WYATT, James (1746-1813). Architect. Born: Staffordshire. His skill at drawing when only fourteen caught the notice of Lord Bagot who, when appointed ambassador to the Papal See, took Wyatt with him to Rome. Returned to London 1766 and did much important work. In 1776 appointed surveyor of Westminster Abbey. President of the Royal Academy of Arts, 1785.

ZUCCARO, Federigo (1543-1609). Painter. An Italian, he came to England in 1574 but only stayed a short while. During the visit he painted Queen Elizabeth, Mary Stuart, etc. The famous portrait of Sir Walter Raleigh in the National Portrait Gallery is believed to be his work.

INDEX

Page references in italics refer to illustrations